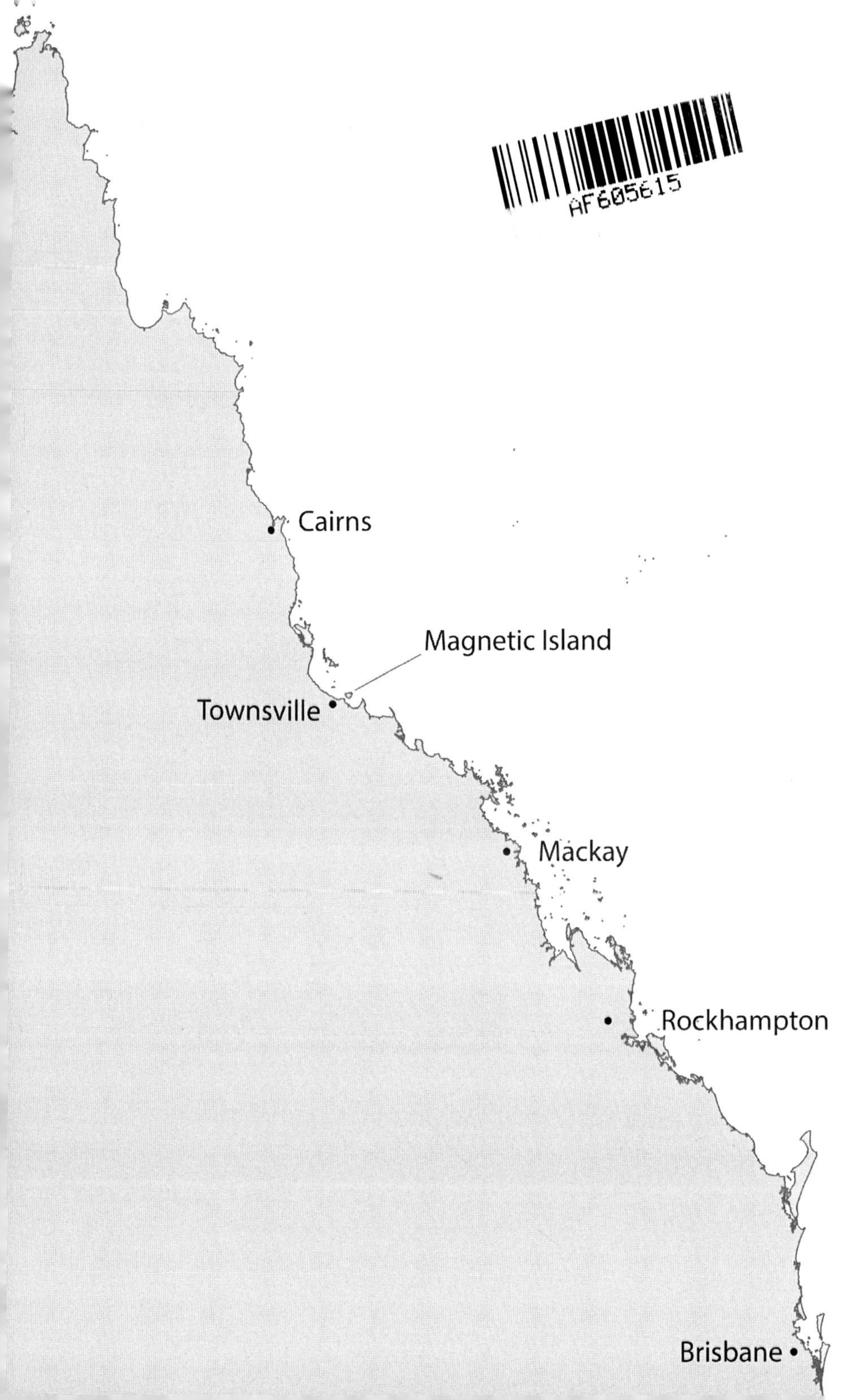
Cairns
Magnetic Island
Townsville
Mackay
Rockhampton
Brisbane

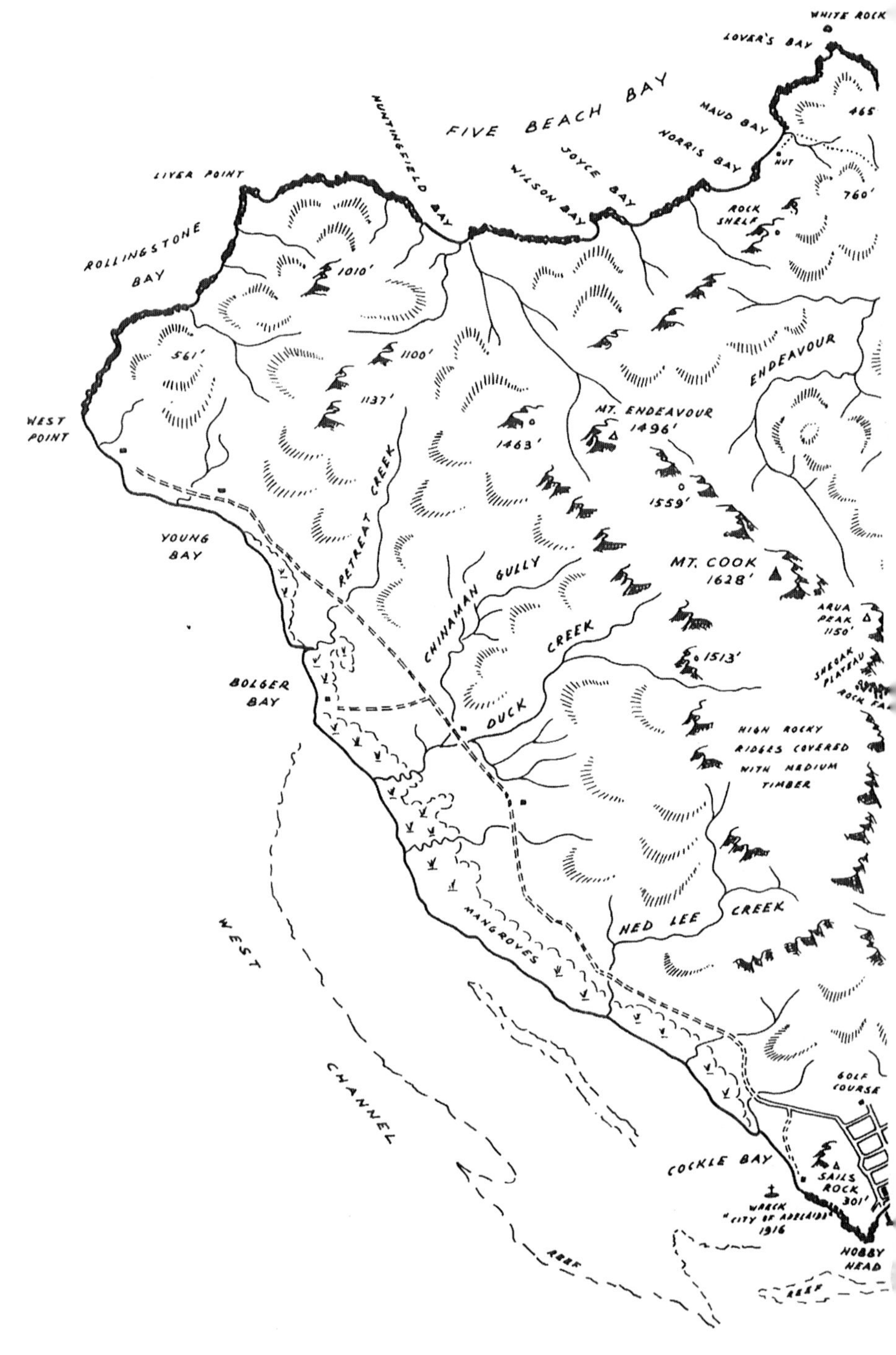

WHITE ROCK
LOVER'S BAY
FIVE BEACH BAY
MAUD BAY
NORRIS BAY
HUT
465'
760'
JOYCE BAY
WILSON BAY
HUNTINGFIELD BAY
LIVER POINT
ROCK SHELF
ROLLINGSTONE BAY
1010'
561'
1100'
1137'
ENDEAVOUR
MT. ENDEAVOUR 1496'
1463'
WEST POINT
1559'
RETREAT CREEK
YOUNG BAY
CHINAMAN GULLY
MT. COOK 1628'
ARUA PEAK 1150'
CREEK
DUCK
1513'
SHEOAK PLATEAU
BOLGER BAY
HIGH ROCKY RIDGES COVERED WITH MEDIUM TIMBER
NED LEE
CREEK
MANGROVES
WEST
CHANNEL
GOLF COURSE
COCKLE BAY
SAILS ROCK 301'
WRECK "CITY OF ADELAIDE" 1916
REEF
NOBBY HEAD
REEF

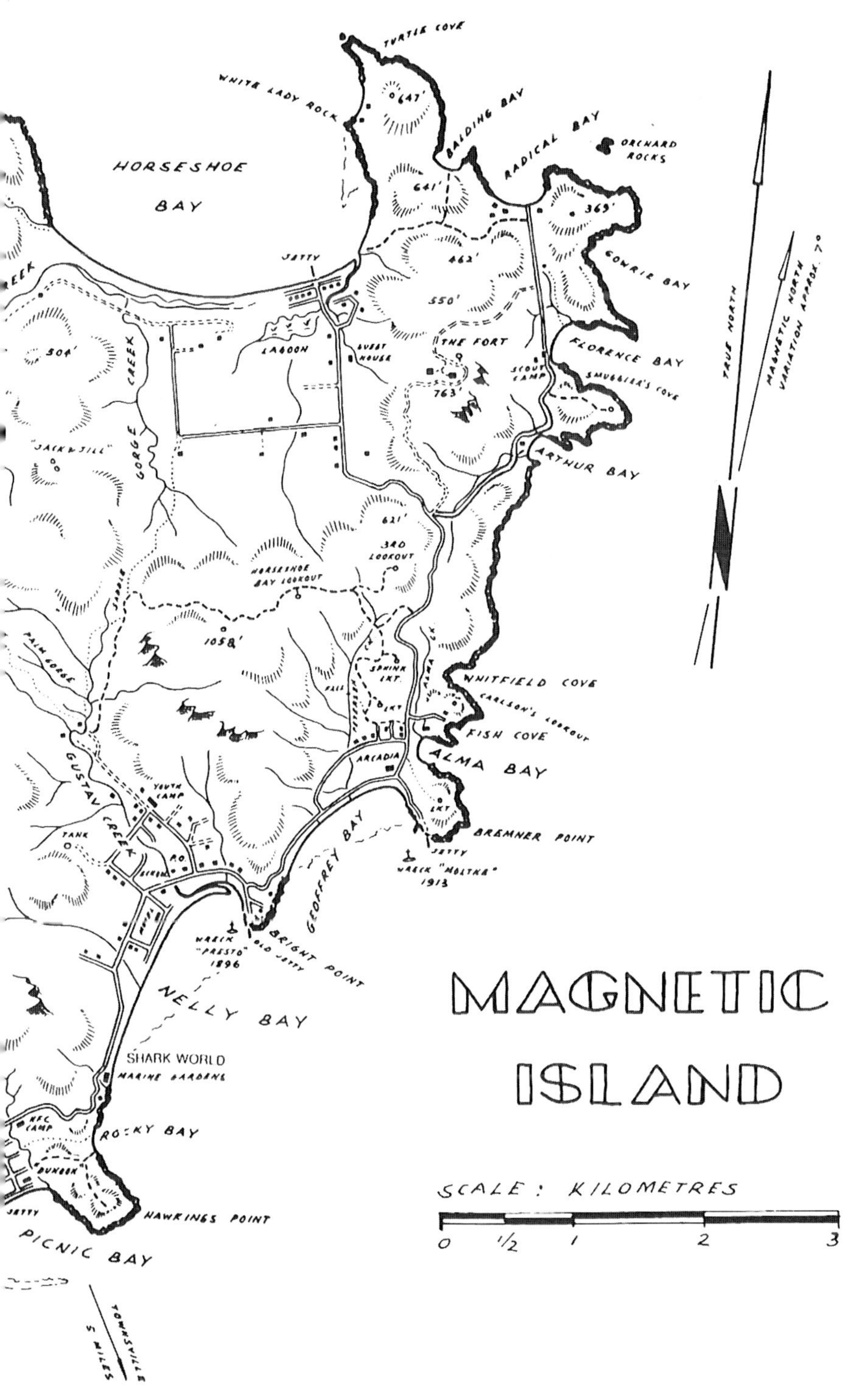

MAGNETIC
ISLAND
SCALE: KILOMETRES
0
1/2
1
2
3
TRUE NORTH
MAGNETIC NORTH
VARIATION APPROX. 7°
TURTLE COVE
WHITE LADY ROCK
647'
HORSESHOE
BAY
BALDING BAY
RADICAL BAY
ORCHARD ROCKS
641'
369'
GOWRIE BAY
JETTY
462'
550'
LAGOON
GUEST HOUSE
THE FORT
763'
SCOUT CAMP
FLORENCE BAY
SMUGGLER'S COVE
ARTHUR BAY
CREEK
GORGE CREEK
504'
"JACK & JILL"
621'
3RD LOOKOUT
HORSESHOE BAY LOOKOUT
1058'
PALM GORGE
SPHINX LKT.
WHITFIELD COVE
CARLSON'S LOOKOUT
FISH COVE
ARCADIA
ALMA BAY
GUSTAV CREEK
YOUTH CAMP
TANK
P.O.
GEOFFREY BAY
LKT
BREMNER POINT
JETTY
WRECK "MOLTKE" 1913
WRECK "PRESTO" 1896
OLD JETTY
BRIGHT POINT
NELLY BAY
SHARK WORLD
MARINE GARDENS
KFC CAMP
ROCKY BAY
BUNKER
JETTY
HAWKINGS POINT
PICNIC BAY
TOWNSVILLE
5 MILES

DISCOVERING MAGNETIC ISLAND

A history and description of Magnetic Island, North Queensland

Other books by James Porter

Fiction
The Swiftlet Isles
Warri of the Wind
The Kumul Feathers
Hapkas Girl
The Sacred Tree
White Water Crossing
Long White Cloud

Non-fiction
Discovering the Family Islands
Edited selections from the
works of E. J . Banfield:
Further Confessions of the Beachcomber
Beachcomber's Paradise

A Family of Islands

DISCOVERING MAGNETIC ISLAND

A history and description of Magnetic Island, North Queensland

JAMES G. PORTER

Illustrated by
KERRIE ATKINS

First published 1983 by Kullari Publication

Revised edition published 1989

Second published 2014 by Boolarong Press

National Library of Australia Cataloguing-in-Publication entry:

Author:	Porter, James, 1929- author.
Title:	Discovering Magnetic Island : a history and description of Magnetic Island, North Queensland / James G. Porter; illustrated by Kerrie Atkins.
ISBN:	9781925046380 (paperback)
Subjects:	Magnetic Island (Qld.)--Description and travel. Magnetic Island (Qld.)--History.
Other Authors/Contributors:	Atkins, Kerrie, illustrator.
Dewey Number:	994.36

Typeset in Arno Pro 12pt.

Illustrations by Kerrie Atkins

Published by Boolarong Press, Salisbury, Brisbane, Australia.

Printed and bound by Watson Ferguson & Company, Salisbury, Brisbane, Australia.

IN MEMORY OF
MARTIN CARLSON

ACKNOWLEDGEMENTS

I would like to acknowledge the use of extracts quoted from Jessie Macqueen's booklet *The Real Magnetic,* published by Willmett & Sons Pty Ltd of Townsville. The quotations from Captain Cook's journals were obtained from the Dr J.C. Beaglehole edited version of *The Journals of Captain James Cook on his voyage of discovery, Volume I.* Much information was gleaned from old newspaper cuttings of the Townsville Daily Bulletin. Other sources were old magazines in the Townsville Public Library, and the staff of the James Cook University Library were helpful with research. Dr George E. Heinsohn of the James Cook University supplied information on the dugong.

I also wish to express appreciation for historical information obtained from the following people during my initial research on the Island prior to 1970. Some of these kindly folk have now passed on: E. R. (Bob) Hayles of Hayles Magnetic Island Pty Ltd., H. G. F. Willmett of Willmett & Sons Pty Ltd., W. J. Laurie, photographer of Townsville, Harry Rouse of Picnic Bay, Clem Ladbury of Radical Bay, Ken Jaffrey of Nelly Bay, Arthur Rollason of Horseshoe Bay, Mrs Janet Mitchell, Mrs K. Cruckshank, Miss M. Dempster of Nelly Bay, and Mrs 'Georgie' Ridge who loaned many of the early photographs of the Butler family. The late Martin Carlson of Fish Cove, Magnetic Island, related many interesting stories of the old days, as did other old-timers mentioned in the text.

Carine Williams and Andree Griffin of the Wildlife Preservation Society of Old, and Jo Wieneke of Nelly Bay, kindly assisted with information on birds.

The pen sketches are by Kerrie Atkins of Picnic Bay. Maps and photographs (other than historical, or where otherwise acknowledged) are my own.

James G. Porter

CONTENTS

The eastern coastline of Magnetic Island

CHAPTER 1
THE MAGNETICAL ISLAND

Magnetic Island has probably never quite outlived Captain Cook's original rather derogatory remarks, made when he first sighted the great hunk of granite-rock and bush sprawled across the mouth of Cleveland Bay. It was June 6th, 1770 when he recorded in his *Endeavour* journal:

> *"This bay which I named Cleveland Bay appear'd to be about 5 or 6 miles in extent every way; the East point I named Cape Cleveland and the West Magnetical Head or Isle as it had much the appearance of an Island and the Compass would not travis well when near it. They are both tolerable high and so is the Mainland within them and the whole appear'd to have the most ruged, rocky and barrenest Surface of any we have yet seen."*

Joseph Banks' comments on the same day are hardly more complimentary:

"Land made in Barren rocky capes; one in particular which we were abreast of in the morn appear'd much like Cape Roxent; at noon 3 fires upon it."

The northeastern corner of Magnetic Island

Banks was referring here to Cook's *Magnetical Head* which Cook referred to elsewhere as *Barren Head*. Cape Roxent is the most westerly point of the European mainland just N.W. of Lisbon. It has been said by some, that Cook actually landed on Magnetic Island, but a detailed examination of his records shows this could not have been possible (see next chapter). Bearings given in his journal make it fairly certain that the closest he approached the Isle would have been a few miles to the north. He was undoubtedly looking at the very steep-sided, rocky, Five Beach Bay coastline, which falls away abruptly in rather bare granite ridges from the high central plateau of Mt Cook.

However, had Cook seen the taller green forests on the southeastern coastline, with its fertile flats and beautiful beaches, he could well have been tempted to make a landing. The Island is only eight kilometres offshore from the present day bustling city of Townsville, the largest population centre in

Australia north of the Tropic of Capricorn. From the mainland, standing on Townsville's Strand and looking out across the bay, the mountainous bulk of land occupying the horizon to the immediate north of the port looks surprisingly almost virgin. The only hint of human settlement is the faint impression of one or two roof-tops showing through the tall eucalypts at Picnic Bay beyond the strip of white sand beach. Yet among its quiet bays live almost two thousand people, many of whom take ad vantage of the regular ferry service to the mainland to commute to work.

The first impression of Magnetic as one approaches in the ferry, is the jumble of huge granite boulders running down to the sea from steep, pine-topped ridges dividing the small sandy bays. These massive weathered rocks stand balanced or wedged precariously between others, all around the Island, while straggling Hoop pine trees gain footholds between crevices, forming a coastline of unique, rugged beauty.

The Island approximates in shape an equilateral triangle of sides eleven to twelve kilometres in length. Roughly seventy per-cent of the total area of 5,100 hectares is National Park reserve. The rest of the Island's acres are available as lease -hold and freehold land for private settlement, unlike most of the other hundreds of islands along Queensland's famous Great Barrier Reef coastline which are, apart from a few select tourist resorts and a handful of rural leases, reserved as National Park areas.

Practically all settlement on Magnetic has occurred on the southeastern to northeastern fringes in separate bay areas, now connected by a bitumen-sealed road winding around the coastline for about fifteen kilometres. Inland, the hills rise to 496 metres at the summit of Mount Cook, centre of the higher land mass comprising National Park. Several creeks carry the water run-off from these forest -clad slopes to the sea on all sides of the Island, the largest of them being Endeavour Creek to the north in Horseshoe Bay, Petersen Creek to the east near Arcadia, Gustav Creek to the southeast in Nelly Bay, and Duck Creek and Ned Lee Creek on the western, mangrove-lined foreshore. These creeks are not perennial. They flow only during the wet season for three or four months each year. The surface water disappears under the sands for the dry season, but can be tapped by wells and bores which have in the past been able to supply most of the Island's needs. Average annual rainfall is 1520 mm.

Water shortages have been alleviated since a water pipe- line was laid across the sea bed from Rowe's Bay on the mainland to Cockle Bay on the Island during 1970, providing reticulated water to residents. Reservoir tanks were sited unobtrusively between folds of the hills behind each settlement. Electric power and telephone submarine cables (both duplicated in case of failure) have also been laid across the bay from the mainland.

The strips of virgin National Park between the individual bays — Picnic, Nelly, Geoffrey, Arcadia and Horseshoe, ensure that development is limited to separate pockets of living areas, leaving plenty of breathing space between. The large area of National Park is insurance for the wildlife, which at the moment enjoys isolation from many mainland hazards. No foxes, dingoes, or predatory man, for firearms are prohibited on the Island. Apart from the prolific bird life there are native rock-wall abies, possums, spiny echidnas (ant-eaters) and koalas. In the quiet evenings — the thump of a rock-wallaby's tail on your lawn; the grunt of a koala from the colony across the creek; the monotonous chop of the nightjar; or the mournful wail of a bush curlew right under the open bedroom window just as you are dozing off ...

The Island seems resilient enough to rejuvenate after the many bushfires and the few cyclones it has suffered. Yet some permanent damage to the flora has been inflicted by fire, and it remains the greatest menace to wildlife and increasingly to man himself, unless there is a greater awareness of the hazards, and indeed, pointlessness of annual burning-off operations. These points have been elaborated in a chapter on the National Park.

The climate is undoubtedly the Magnetic Isle's biggest attraction, for at latitude 19 degrees South, it is nicely enough positioned to capitalize on a balmy winter, and though there is tropical heat and humidity in summer, it does not experience the dry dust and extreme temperature ranges of the inland, with the milder, moister influence of the bordering Pacific Ocean to bring cooling sea breezes.

The Magnetical Island today, in spite of increasing tourism, is still a place where the quieter influences of nature can intrude delightfully into everyday life. And it is a place with a past, a place where in the lazy warmth, sitting contemplating the ancient weathered granite sculptures standing sentinel over the beaches, one may find oneself, as did poet Jessie Macqueen, taking up a little of the 'Island Dreaming'.

"Ageless-you have turned many a page

In book of time, while we engage

A few short years, then life is done

But you eternally are young

Holding us in your spell.

Dream Magnetic, of ages past

Dream, but tell us your dreams at last ... "

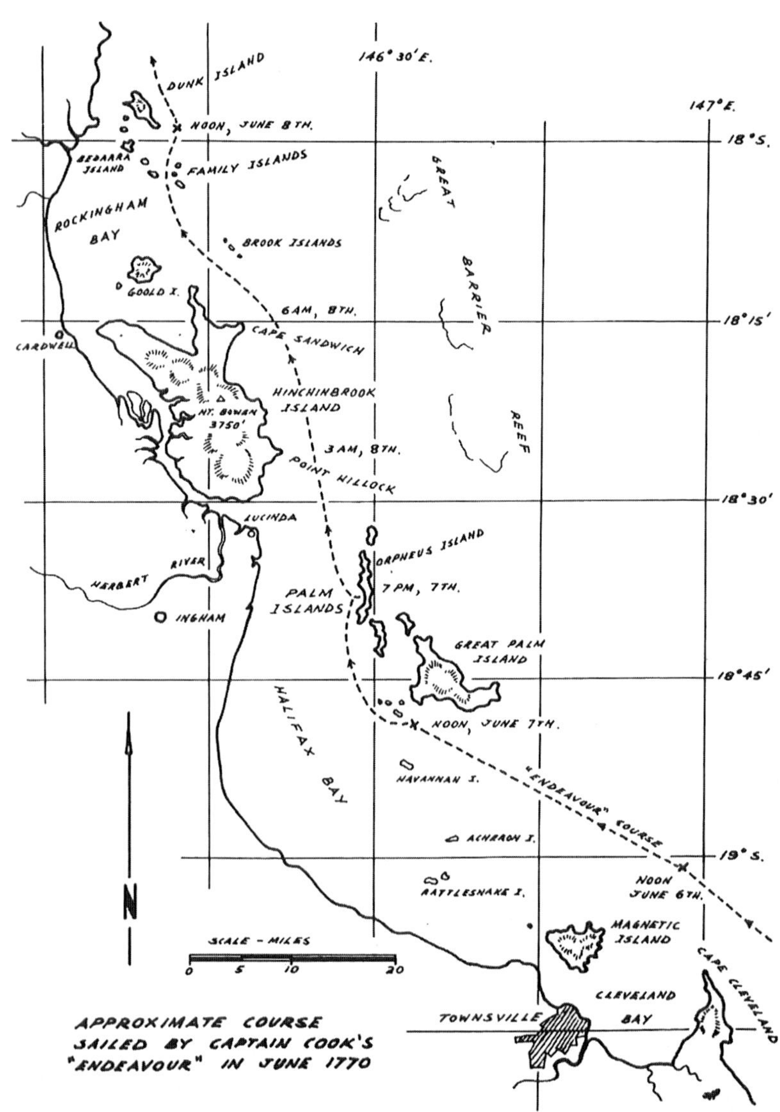

APPROXIMATE COURSE SAILED BY CAPTAIN COOK'S "ENDEAVOUR" IN JUNE 1770

CHAPTER 2
CAPTAIN COOK

In day of old, the Captain bold,

On board the barque, Endeavour,

Found Cleveland Bay magnetical —

The charm remains for ever.

Viator

Did Captain Cook or any of his party land on Magnetic Island? To answer that question let us look closely at the most authentic present-day copy of Cook's journals — the Dr. J. C. Beaglehole edited version, *The Journals of Captain James Cook on his voyage of discovery, Volume I.*

"Wednesday, June 6th. Light airs at ESE with which we steer'd WNW as the land now lay, depth of water 12 & 14 fathoms. At Noon we were by Observation in the Latitude of 19°1'. Longitude made from Cape Gloucester 1°30' west, Course

and distance sail'd sence yesterday noon WNW 28 Miles. In this situation we had the mouth of a bay all open extending from the S½E to SW½S distant 2 Leagues. This bay which I named Cleveland Bay appear'd to be about 5 or 6 Miles in extent every way; the East point I named Cape Cleveland and the West Magnetical Head or Isle as it had much the appearance of an Island and the Compass would nor travis well when near it. They are both tolerable high and so is the Mainland within them and the whole appear'd to have the most ruged, rocky and barrenest Surface of any we have yet seen. However it is not without inhabitants as we saw smooks in several places in the bottom of the Bay. The northernmost land we had in sight at this time bore NW, this we took to be an Island or Islands for we could not trace the Main land further than WBN."

Now the bearings given above of the "mouth of a bay all open extending from the S½E to SW½S distant 2 Leagues" (a league is approximately 3 miles) together with the given latitude 19°1'S. (the latitude of the northern coast of Magnetic Island is 19 °8'S. and Cook's latitude observations would have been quite accurate, though longitude calculations could be doubtful due to the inaccurate chronometers of his day) put the Endeavour approximately seven miles N.E. of the north-eastern corner of Magnetic Island at that time, noon. This also tallies with his soundings of 12 and 14 fathoms, which occur well out to sea on the latest marine chart of Cleveland Bay area: Cook's reference to Magnetical Head or Isle indicates that he was not even sure it was an island, a fact he would surely have verified had he landed, for the closest point of the mainland to the Island is more than three miles. The last part of his journal entry for the 6th describing "the northernmost land we had in sight at this time bore. NW" was obviously in reference to the Palm Islands.

The Five Beach Bay coastline, the northern face of the Island which Captain Cook saw

At this point in the original journal, Dr. Beaglehole notes an interesting little sidelight. He says that Cook deleted an additional sentence which does not appear in any of the copies of Cook's journal:

> *"Notwithstanding we have been long in soundings, have had it frequently calm and been often at an Anchor we have caught no fish worth mentioning sence we left Sting-Ray Harbour."*

Continuing the extracts from Cook's journal: —

> *"Thursday, June 7th. Light airs between the South and East with which we steered WNW, keeping the Main land on board the outermost part of which at sun set bore from us WBN, but without this lay high land which we took to be Islands. At day light in the morning we were the length of the Eastern part of this land which we found to consist of a group of Islands laying about 5 Leagues from the Main we being at this time between the two; we continued advancing slowly to the NW until! Noon at which time we were by observation in*

the Latitude of 18°49' and about 5 Leagues from the Main land, the Northwest part of which bore from us NBW½W the Island extending from the North to East, distant off the nearest 2 Miles; Cape Cleveland bore S50° East distant 18 Leagues. Our sounding in the Course of this days sail were from 14 to 11 fathom."

An important point to be remembered when reading Cook's journals is that he used "ship's time" or "sea-time" by which each day begins at midday on the preceding day according to "civil-time". Thus the first entry for Thursday 7th, describing sun-set, really refers to the afternoon or P.M. of Wednesday 6th, and "daylight in the morning" a little further on refers to the Thursday morning.

Thus for the rest of the afternoon of Wednesday 6th they steered W.N.W. past the northern face of Magnetic Island, making for a course between the Palm Islands (30 miles north of Magnetic) and the mainland. The wind was very light that afternoon, so light in fact that Banks was able to go out a little way in the small boat that evening to shoot birds. This is noted from the extract from Joseph Banks' journal which follows later, but no reference is yet made to anchoring or going ashore. On the ·following morning of Thursday 7th, they were approaching the Palm Islands and at noon that day they were already at latitude 18°49' S. near the southern end of present day Great Palm Island, according to the bearings given of both the Island and Cape Cleveland in the distance. This is about 30 miles N.N.W. of Magnetic Island.

Let Captain Cook continue his narrative: —

*"**Friday, June 8th**. Winds at SSE and South first part light airs the remainder a gentle breeze. In the PM we saw several large smooks upon the main, some people Canoes and as we thought Cocoa-nutt Trees upon one of the Islands, and as a*

few of these nutts would have been very acceptable to us at this time I sent Lieut. Hicks a Shore with whome went Mr. Banks and Dr. Solander to see what was to be got, in the mean time we kept standing in for the Island with the Ship. At 7 o'clock they returnd on board having met with nothing worth observing, the trees we saw were small kind of Cabbage Palms; they heard some of the Natives as they were putting off from the shore but saw none. After the boats were hoisted in we stood away NBW for the northernmost land we had in sight which we were abreast off at 3 o'clock in the Morning having past all the Islands 3 or 4 hours before; this point I have named Point Hillock ..."

H M Brig ENDEAVOUR

length 30 metres
weight 368 tons

Cook's entry' "In the PM" here refers to the Thursday afternoon of the 7th. It was only then that he saw *Cocoa-nutt Trees* on one of the islands and sent Lieut. Hicks ashore with Banks and Solander. It is obvious that this particular reference to landing was to one of the Palm Islands (actually his charts and times seem to indicate that it was Orpheus Island, one of the northern Palm group, which would also tally with the fact that he was off Great Palm Island at midday and would have had plenty of time to reach Orpheus before evening) for within a further eight hours (between 7pm and 3am) they were abreast of Point Hillock on present day Hinchinbrook Island (Cook was not aware that the great towering mass of 3,000 foot high peaks on the mainland side of him was an island) having as Cook says, "passed all the Islands 3 or 4 hours before". Point Hillock is approximately 80 miles north of Magnetic; rather stretching things too much for the sailing capabilities of the old Endeavour in eight hours in light winds, if the island visited was Magnetic.

There is a further interesting complication in the matter of Captain Cook's time reckoning, which is not generally taken into account. This is the fact that when Cook crossed the 180th Meridian of longitude (the International Date Line) on his way westwards across the Pacific, he made no adjustment to the dates in his log and journal, and therefore all the dates referred to while he was on the east coast of Australia, should be advanced by one full day to give correct chronology. Therefore although Cook recorded it as the 6th when he sighted Magnetic Island, it was in fact June 7th.

The following extract from Joseph Banks' Endeavour journals substantiate the fact that the only island visited by them in this vicinity was one in the Palm group.

*"**June 6th**. Land made in Barren rocky capes; one in particular which we were abreast of in the morn appear'd much like Cape Roxent; at noon 3 fires upon it. Many Cuttle bones, Some sea weed and 2 or 3 Sea snakes were seen. In the evening it fell quite calm and I went out in the small boat and shot nectris nugax (Dusky or Audubon's Shearwater) but saw nothing remarkable on the water; the weather most sultry hot in an open boat.*

June 7th. *Sailing between the main and islands; (the Palm Islands) the main rose steep from the water rocky and barren. Just about sun rise a shoal of fish about the size of and much like flounders but perfectly white went by the ship. At noon the islands had mended their appearance and people were seen upon them; the Main as barren as ever with several fires upon it, one vastly large. After dinner an appearance very much like Cocoanut trees tempted us to hoist out a boat and go ashore, where we found our supposed Cocoanut trees to be no more than bad Cabbage trees. (Livistona Australis) The Countrey about them was very stoney and barren and it was almost dark when we got ashore; we made a shift however to gather 14 or 15 new plants after which we repaired to our boats but scarce were they put off from the shore when an Indian came very near it and shouted to us very loud ; it was so dark that we could not see him, we however turned towards the shore by way of seeing what he wanted with us, but he I suppose ran away or hid himself immediately for we could not get a sight of him."*

Banks is obviously using civil -time in his journal, for the visit ashore was referred to as "after dinner" on June 7th, whereas in Cook's journal this reference appears as PM of June 8th ship's time.

It remains a mystery as to why Cook thought the Island to be "magnetic". He said that his compass was affected, yet no magnetic anomaly has ever since been recorded in the vicinity of Magnetic Island. Actually the main reference to this disturbance was made in his journal on June 5th, the day before reaching the Island. Cook recorded:

> *"At sun· rise I found the variation to be 5°35' Easterly; at sun set last night the same Needle gave near go. This being close under Cape Upstart, I judged that it was owing to Iron Ore or other Magnetical matter lodged in the earth."*

Cape Upstart is 80 miles south-east of Magnetic Island and no magnetic anomaly exists there either. In 1892 an expedition under A. Gibb Maitland of the Queensland Geology Department, examined Magnetic Island very thoroughly, but was unable to determine the reason for the influence on Cook's compass. They found the Island to consist mainly of granite and quartz reefs. It has been suggested that perhaps a re-arrangement of cannon or other iron-ware on board the Endeavour unbeknown to Cook, could have been the cause of his compass disturbance.

However the name for the Island has stuck, much to the convenience of present day tourist promoters who revel in the cliche, "the Magnetic attraction" of this tropic isle.

Harold Butler, first settler on Magnetic Island 1877

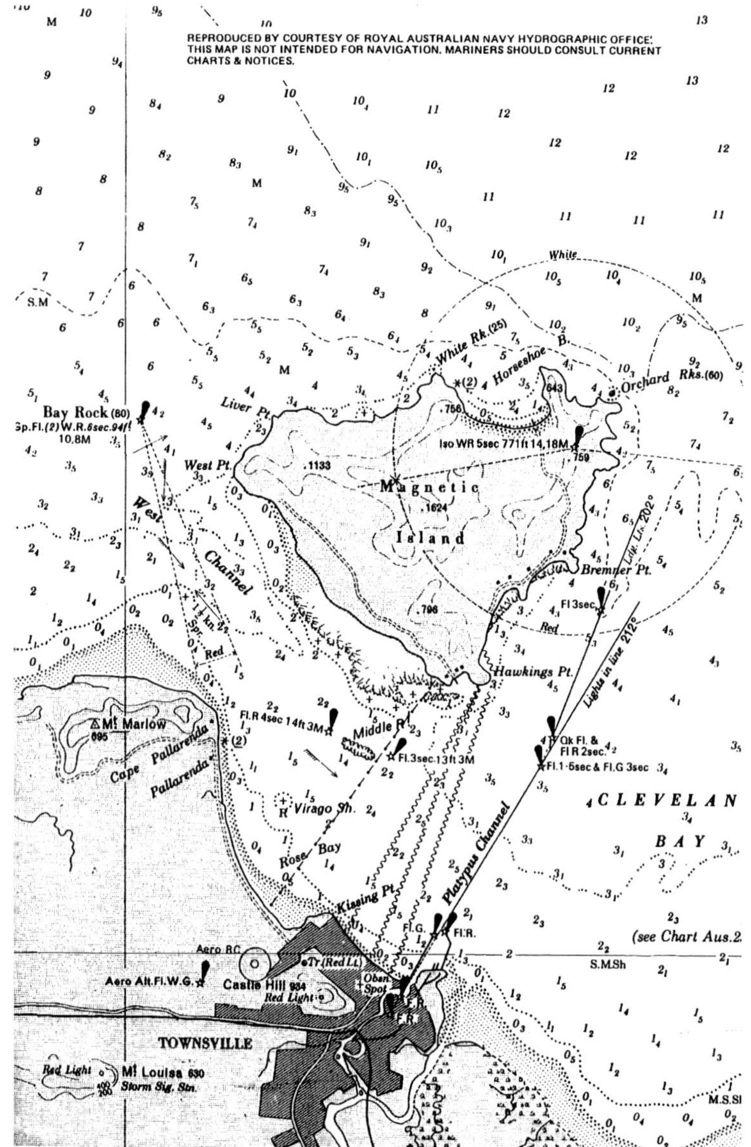

REPRODUCED BY COURTESY OF ROYAL AUSTRALIAN NAVY HYDROGRAPHIC OFFICE. THIS MAP IS NOT INTENDED FOR NAVIGATION. MARINERS SHOULD CONSULT CURRENT CHARTS & NOTICES.
White Rk. (25)
Horseshoe B.
Orchard Rks. (60)
Bay Rock (80)
Gp.Fl.(2) W.R.6sec.94ft 10.8M
Liver Pt.
West Pt.
Magnetic Island
Iso WR 5sec 771ft 14,18M
West Channel
Bremner Pt.
Fl 3sec.
Red
Hawkings Pt.
Ldg. Lts. 202°
Lights in line 212°
M! Marlow
Cape Pallarenda
Pallarenda
Fl.R 4sec 14ft 3M
Middle R.
Fl.3sec.13ft 3M
Qk Fl. & Fl R 2sec.
Fl.1·5sec & Fl.G 3sec
CLEVELAND BAY
Virago Sh.
Rose Bay
Kissing Pt.
Platypus Channel
Fl.G.
Fl.R.
(see Chart Aus.2
Aero BC
Tr (Red Lt.)
Aero Alt.Fl.W.G.
Castle Hill 934
Red Light
Obsn Spot
F.R.
S.M.Sh
TOWNSVILLE
Red Light
M! Louisa 630
Storm Sig. Stn.
M.S.Sl

CHAPTER 3
PIONEERS

Magnetic Island, like the mainland, had its population of Aborigines wandering from bay to bay. Native canoes plyed regularly across the channel separating West Point from Cape Pallarenda on the mainland, as the earliest pioneers observed. There are signs of Aboriginal middens remaining today - for example there is one in Florence Bay where oyster shells were left in large numbers. Early white residents were also aware of native camps and watering places behind Arcadia settlement and along the West Point track which was their last refuge. Some mainland tribes used to wade out to the channel from Kissing Point, Townsville, during the low Spring tides, swimming the last lap to the Island reef, to hunt and gossip with their Island friends.

The Island had much to offer the Aboriginal. Apart from the plentiful supply of fish and oysters around its shores there were edible roots and reed bulbs growing in the swamps around Horseshoe Bay and Nelly Bay; plants described as the bulgaroo or swamp-nut and the pincara bulb, the latter being poisonous until specially treated in the way they knew. It was pounded into a flat, doughy state until it resembled moist white bread, which kept well while being carried around in their dilly-bags. The numerous rock -wallabies were a source of meat. Everything in the bush had its uses, and Magnetic was more bountiful than the mainland in many ways. Burdekin plum trees gave their fruit, Pandanus nuts had their edible cores after soaking and roasting, and giant ti-trees growing in the creek beds provided layers of soft, tissue-like paper -bark which could be put to so many uses, not least as a wrapping for their new born babes.

It seems that the Queensland coast was visited by Europeans even before Captain Cook, for traces of a Spanish village and shipwreck were reputed to have been found near Gladstone, though it was apparently not occupied long. An early settler at Gladstone who accompanied the original surveying party to lay out the township in 1853, recorded that they found embedded in the sand at South Trees Point, a brass cannon which was in a good state of preservation and inscribed "Santa Barbara, 1596". This coincided with theories developed by Lawrence Hargrave, the aviation pioneer, who said that the *Santa Barbara* was a small caravel sent from Manila to search for a previous deserter from Mendana's fleet in 1595 which it was thought had gone searching for gold in the Great South Land.

Following Captain Cook's map-making expedition in 1770 and his near disastrous shipwreck on the treacherous Barrier Reef, few Europeans took any interest in this part of the coast for 42 years. Ships generally passed outside the Reef, including that of Matthew Flinders on his northern surveying trips. Not until 1812 were ships to use the inner route, when Captain Cripps of the brig *Cyclops* sailed through, and also Lieutenant Jeffreys of the brig *Kangaroo*, who was forced inside the reef by bad weather, to eventually land at Goold Island north of Hinchinbrook. There may have been other unrecorded passages, but Captain Phillip King (R.N.), one-time governor of N.S.W., surveyed the Cleveland Bay and Magnetical Island area in 1819 in the small cutter *Mermaid*, sending ashore a party to the Island. Lieutenant John Stokes of HMS *Beagle*, who became well known for his Northern Territory discoveries, stayed at Magnetic Island for five days in June 1841 to test his chronometers.

One wonders whether the ship-wrecked mariner, 23 year-old James Morrill, who was washed ashore on Cape Cleveland in 1846 and survived for 17 years with kindly blackfellows, ever visited Magnetic Island during his walkabouts with the tribe. His ship the *Peruvian* was wrecked on the Barrier Reef after leaving Sydney on February 27, 1846. Sixteen men, three women and two children managed to leave the wreck on a raft, to drift for 42 days before landing on the southern point of Cape Cleveland. Only seven people survived the raft voyage and two more died on the beach within a few days. Local Aborigines took them in hand, Morrill and a young boy being claimed by a Mt. Elliott tribe, and Captain Pitkethly and his wife going to a Cape Cleveland tribe. Two years later Morrill was the only survivor. During the following years various ships were seen but could not be attracted, or if they were, it was for the 'blacks' to be shot at. In 1863 when Morrill approached shepherds at an outstation hut of Anthill's run, he was burned almost black from the sun and could hardly speak English. He died only two years after rescue at the age of 41.

The fact that Morrill's experience lasted until 1863 would seem to indicate that Cleveland Bay was not visited by anyone else up to that time, not even by those strange whalers and pirate -drifters of the period who sailed the Pacific area for what they could exploit. However, during the early years of

Townsville's settlement from 1864 on, there were obviously many temporary visits by white men to Magnetic Island: fishermen setting traps and nets, or merely adventurers looking at the lay of the land.

Although Harry Butler is the most well known pioneer associated with the Island's early history, the first man to take more than a passing interest in Magnetic was, as far as can be ascertained, a Mr Cocksfield during the early 1870's. This information was derived from an account recorded in the *Townsville Evening Star* of Saturday, November 7th, 1931, of a broadcast over radio 4TO by W. E. Mcllwaine, president of the Townsville Chamber of Commerce. Part of his address was as follows:

> "It is always interesting to record the name of the first white settler in any new land. I, therefore, went to some trouble to find out to whom the honour in this case is due. From the information I have, it seems that away back in the early 70's a Mr and Mrs Cocksfield settled in Nelly Bay, and engaged in felling pine-trees and rafting the logs to Townsville. These logs were used in building the new town, then in its in fancy. A story is told of Mrs Cocksfield putting to sea on a pine log to escape the blacks, who threatened trouble during the absence of her husband. After the finish of the timber-getting activities of the Cocksfields, the Island lay unoccupied by white people until 1887, when Mr and Mrs Harry Butler and family arrived and settled in Picnic Bay."

From the well authenticated information which follows, it is clear that the date 1887 referred to above concerning Harry Butler, should have been 1877. Perhaps it is a printer's error in the paper because in the same article Mr Mcllwaine refers to Harry Butler's brother Joe, coming to Nelly Bay in 1884.

Harold Butler, a Lancashireman, was undoubtedly the first to take up permanent residence on Magnetic Island. Like Mrs Cocksfield, he also came into early startling contact with the Aborigines. He sailed across the Bay from Townsville late one afternoon alone in a small boat, to explore the Isle for a possible home-site, and with the swift onset of tropical darkness soon after he reached the forested shores, he decided to sleep on the warm beach sands at Picnic Bay for the night. Next morning young Harold was awakened from his slumber by the voices of six naked blackfellows standing over him, armed with spears and nulla null as. Surprised but unflustered, he reckoned they were not hostile — at least he reasoned they had contacted plenty of white men before and were merely curious at the sight of a white-fella roughing it on the beach. With a little sign language and an understanding twinkle in his eye, Harry Butler straightaway cemented a friendship with the Aborigines which was to last for the rest of his long life on the Isle.

Harry Butler's story is told delightfully by Jessie Macqueen in her booklet, *The Real Magnetic,* one of the few documents available on the early history of the Island. Miss Macqueen was an intimate friend of the Butler family and although she lived in Townsville, she visited the Island often to be with Nellie, Harry's daughter. Apart from her literary interests (she wrote poetry and published another booklet called *Memories of Townsville*) Jessie Macqueen became known for other talents considered unusual for a woman. She was a crack-shot at the Rifle Range, winning trophies against male shooters, and was a foundation member of the Townsville Ladies Rowing Club which during World War I conducted rowing regattas to raise funds for charities. With her sister Leila she once rowed the five miles from Ross Creek, Townsville to Picnic Bay in a 14 foot dinghy. She often climbed in the Mt. Spec Ranges north of Townsville and also climbed to the summit of Mt. Cook on Magnetic Island with Nellie Butler, an incident decribed later.

Jessie Macqueen came to Townsville as an infant, having been born at Omeo, Victoria in 1879. Her father, an accountant, was a Scottish Canadian from Prince Edward Island, Canada, who was persuaded by a friend to go to Townsville as the up and coming city of Queensland. He went into partnership with John Marshall in a second-hand bookshop, trading as Marshal! & Macqueen, Booksellers & Accountants, in a shop near the present Excelsior Hotel in Flinders Street. The Macqueens lived at the Ross Is land settlement in Townsville in a dusty little street called Palmer Street, surrounded by thick mangroves and muddy backwaters. They had no such things as water taps and when dry seasons came, water was carted in casks on an old wagon drawn by draught-horses, at a cost of 2/6 per gallon.

Later, Jessie herself owned a bookselling business in Flinders Street on a site now occupied by the Bank of N.S.W. In 1927 she sold out and went to Sydney, but returned to Townsville in 1951 to live in retirement on the Strand. She wrote both her booklets then, but earlier had written a prize winning ode in a Sydney *Sunday Sun* competition, and had a number of children's poems published in the *Adelaide News* in 1927. She died on 17th May, 1966 at the age of 87.

Her booklet *The Real Magnetic* describes how Harry Butler migrated from Lancashire as a young man with his family in 1867, intending originally to join his brother Charlie, already settled at Cardwell. As their ship the *Royal Dane* passed close by Magnetic Island on the way in to Townsville, Harry Butler was much impressed by the wild, green island, evidently much more so than Captain Cook had been. As he told Jessie Macqueen years later, "I liked the look of it. And I made up my mind then and there to settle on this little island. Brother Charlie of course tried to persuade me to go to Cardwell , but as I say I got a sort of feeling for Magnetic and nothing would change me."

Nell Butler, after whom Nelly Bay was named

Following a few early jobs in Townsville and five years in Mackay, where in 1872 Mrs Butler gave birth to another daughter, Ellen ('Nellie', Jessie Macqueen's friend to be), Harry returned to Townsville to take on fencing work in order to support his family. One of his jobs was to erect a post and railing fence around the present Botanical Gardens. His last job under a boss was digging rock-coral from the reef near his dreamland, Magnetic. Some of this rock bui lt Townsville's first small court-house.

Harry Butler soon bought himself a small sailing boat called *Lady of the Lake,* which name it is presumed he changed to *Enterprise* because other references give the latter as the name of his first boat. In this vessel he ventured off alone that afternoon already described, to explore the bush-clad mountains and clean sand beaches of his Isle. He described tall forests stretching from the mountain tops to the very edges of its many beaches. He also noted wild dogs, yellowish in colour but not true dingo according to him. There are none on the Island now. The pleasant strip of sand at Picnic Bay facing towards Townsville across the water was his choice of all the virgin bays - the place where he eventually brought his wife and children to live.

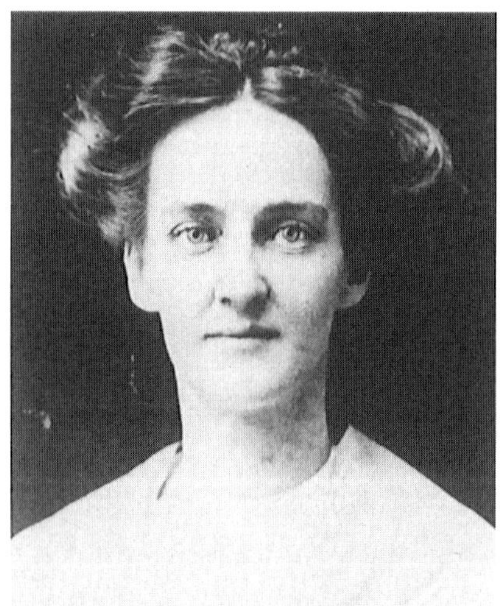

Jessie Macqueen in the costume of the Townsville Ladies Rowing Club, during World War I

In the beginning the Butler family became involuntarily associated with the first quarantine procedures adopted by embarrassed authorities for an increasing number of overseas immigrant ships arriving at the Port of Townsville. These ships would anchor in Cleveland Bay flying the yellow flag to call for health officials from the port, then when cases of typhoid or other dreadful diseases picked up on the voyage were discovered, the patients were rowed ashore to Picnic Bay to be quarantined in tents near the beach until they either recovered or died. After a doctor had done all he could, Mrs Butler and her daughters succoured the unfortunate women at the eastern end of the Bay near Hawking's Point, while Harry and his sons tendered to the men segregated at the other end of the beach near the present day baths and Surf Life Saving Club premises, on what is now known as Knobby Point.

'Grandad' Butler with Jessie Macqueen (left) and Nell Butler prior to 1920

When the inevitable happened and a number of these unlucky migrants died, Harry Butler was called upon to assume the role of both clergyman and undertaker at the burial services. Six persons were buried near where the present Hotel Magnetic now stands, .and other strange graves appeared in various parts of the Bay. A beautiful 19 year-old girl, to whom the family became very attached, was buried sadly right alongside the Butler home.

Will Fraser and Nell (nee Butler)

Eventually a proper quarantine station was erected at the far western corner of the Island near West Point, with a resident official to take charge of things. Later again this was removed to a more convenient site on the mainland opposite at Cape Pallarenda, leaving nature to cleanse the Magnetical Isle with her salubrious sea-breezes and bright sunshine.

An article in the *Townsville Daily Bulletin* of April 23rd, 1936, recorded an interview with Harry Butler's daughter Emma, then Mrs E. Gray living in Townsville, who recalled many of the family's early pioneering efforts on Magnetic. She said that the family's coming to settle there fulfilled an English crystal-gazer's prophecy that Mrs Butler would live on an island.

Emma was four years old when her parents first arrived in Australia in 1867, and ten years later they settled in Picnic Bay. She retained vivid memories of helping her father carry great bricks of coral which had been cut from the sea-bed, across the sandy beach to the site of their first house under the trees. With bare feet sinking into the burning sand, the whole family struggled with their individual burdens as contribution to their new home. At 14 years of age, Emma helped dig a well at Picnic Bay during a dry spell, and as any well-digger knows that is no mean task for a young girl.

During those early times bad weather often held them up for days when sailing to or from the mainland in their small boat. Emma recalled one occasion before they were properly established, when the family came near to starvation after Harry was prevented from returning to the Island with essential stores during a prolonged spell of rough weather. They were reduced to foraging (unsuccessfully) for food with the blacks. After rationing the last of the food one night, Mrs Butler finally broke down and wept in front of her children. Emma rushed outside because she could not bear to see her mother crying. Suddenly in the evening air she heard the familiar sound of anchor chains from across the water, and there in the moonlight was the dark shape of her father's boat, luffing to an anchorage in the bay.

Another time Harry Butler was marooned at the Island end with his boat. Emma was at school in Townsville then, and when no news was heard from the family for some time after boisterous weather, a friend, Mr Charles Norris, took his powerful binoculars down to the foreshore to focus them on

Picnic Bay across the water. He saw the boat lying on its side on the beach with a big hole in the hull and promptly sent aid. During further escapades the Butlers rowed a dinghy all the way across to the mainland, or spent up to four or five hours standing into a stiff northerly in the little sail-boat before reaching home.

When Harry really started settling in, completing his house of coral, sand and limestone on the spot now occupied by "Dunoon" Guest House, establishing an orchard, rearing poultry and pigs and acquiring a small dairy herd swum ashore from a cargo steamer, he replaced his first boat with a larger sailing vessel, the *Hepziba,* 28 feet long. In this, his seven children were taken over to school in Townsville to board with friends. They enrolled at the Central, then South Townsville state school. Eventually guests were brought over in the *Hepziba* to holiday at the guest cabins he constructed with thatched roofs. A wooden jetty, later known as 'Butler's Jetty' to distinguish it from Hayles' jetty, was made for the convenience of landing both passengers and goods. A horse and cart completed the Butler Guest House complex.

The establishment became very popular over the years, with weekend visitors arriving on the beach in sailing boats or from big steamers moored offshore, bringing an increasing number of 'picnickers' to give the bay its name. In 1903 the *Hepziba* was sold to the Yarrabah Mission just south of Cairns and was eventually wrecked on nearby Fitzroy Island. Harry Butler then bought the *Tivoli,* the first motor vessel in Townsville which was used for private charter work as well as on the Island passenger service for many years.

Harry Butler was sympathetic toward the various wayward wanderers who turned up on the shores of Magnetic Island during the early years. Escaped convicts from New Caledonia or other distant places often drifted ashore at Nelly Bay or Rocky Bay after a drift of hundreds of miles on the ocean currents through gaps in the Reef, their vessel a make-shift raft or stolen dinghy. A starving skeleton staggering over the ridge from the eastern beaches to Butler's house in Picnic Bay, would be fed and restored to life before being taken to the mainland in the *Hepziba* hidden under a pile of sails. There, they were released to become free or re-captured, as luck would have it, but Harry reckoned that it wasn't for him to judge them. Many men were sent to those convict settlements for purely political reasons, others for harmless crimes.

The Butlers were sometimes innocent pawns in more serious breaches of the migration and smuggling laws. Opium found its way ashore from 'fishing' boats working in the Bay close to anchoring overseas ships. One particular incident involved illegal entry of Japanese people to the mainland via Magnetic, although the family would never have realized this had it not been for a Sunday School picnic party in Rocky Bay. The youngsters on returning home at the end of the day recounted to Nell Butler a wild story of three dark-skinned 'gypsies' in Rocky Bay, hiding among the rocks and trees. Their tale was scoffed at good-humouredly by the family who reckoned they must have seen sun-burned bathers from the main land playing hide and seek .

For some time prior to this incident the Butlers had been visited regularly by a friendly Japanese 'sight-seer' whenever his ship was in harbour. The day after the Sunday School picnic, a day of high winds and rough seas, when visitors from the mainland were few, the same man accompanied by three other Japanese including a woman, walked unexpectedly over the hill from Rocky Bay to Butler's house. Smiling and bowing, their previous visitor explained that big seas had swamped their fishing boat hired from the mainland, and forced them ashore at Rocky Bay with no means of returning to town. Accepting their story that they were only picnickers, Harry's son George took them all ashore in the *Hepziba*. In return for this kindness the Japanese woman offered Nell a gold ring which she smilingly refused. Nell also refused the man's offer to send over a roll of silk from Townsville.

Not until some months afterwards did the full significance of that episode become apparent. Will Fraser, Nell's husband, while climbing about the rocks in Rocky Bay one day, discovered the remains of a collapsible iron framework canvas canoe which had been deliberately destroyed there. Memory of the Sunday School picnic and the youngsters' story of 'gypsies' in the woods followed by the Japanese visitors soon afterwards prompted him to put two and two together. The canoe had obviously carried those four Japanese straight to the Island from a vessel in harbour.

Standing high above the western ridge of the Picnic Bay skyline, silhouetted in bold outline, is a huge granite boulder - a vertical slab protruding above its rocky foundation, forming a well -known landmark. Harry Butler named it "Sails Rock" after a young sailmaker who deserted ship in Cleveland Bay. "Sails" had apparently been ill -treated on board his vessel and had decided to jump ship at the first opportunity. When his ship anchored in the Bay one afternoon to load stores from punts putting out from Townsville in the days before the port had a wharf, "Sails" was ordered to paint the ship's sides. While standing in a small boat alongside wielding the paint brush he noticed how close they were to Cockle Bay on Magnetic Island. Grabbing the oars he pushed off straight for the mangroves, but halfway across was seen by the Captain. A shot rang out, but whether the Captain's aim was poor, or he was merely trying to bluff "Sails" into returning, the lad didn't stop to find out. Each burst of gunfire spurred him on to superhuman efforts on the oars and he rushed into the mangroves to scramble out barefooted and climb the rocky peninsula behind the Bay.

Pursued by a party from the ship he climbed high up the steep slopes through prickly vines and thick bush, to hide right under the summit in a cavern. There he remained motionless until nightfall, while his not too energetic followers soon gave up the search and towed his boat back to the ship. Next morning after a sleepless night "Sails" noticed the ship still anchored there waiting . He also saw the Butler's house down on the other side of the ridge in Picnic Bay, but dared not go down there with the ship still in the Bay. He spent a thirsty day under the big rock nursing his sore feet.

When late in the afternoon his ship up-anchored and sailed over the horizon, the lad climbed down to make straight for the light from Butler's house. Thoroughly weakened by thirst he was hardly able to stagger within earshot. His cries in the darkness were heard by the family who, armed with lanterns eventually found him in the bush. Ever after when "Grandad" related that tale, it was to refer to "Sails Rock".

About a mile past Cockle Bay on the West Point track is a pleasant, shady watercourse, bordered by tall gums and ti-trees, known as Ned Lee's Creek, which in good seasons runs with clear water for many months. Ned Lee was an Irishman who made friends with the last sad remnants of the blackfellows at their camp on the banks of this creek. Eventually he married one of the gins of the tribe and lived with her people there for many years. One day Harry Butler was approached by a couple of long-faced tribesmen from the camp who told him, "Ned, he go bung — Ned, he altogether finish." Harry, with a spade on his shoulder and a bible in his hand, accompanied them back to the camp for a burial service-the last he was to perform on the Island.

Up in the hills along Ned Lee's Creek is an abandoned gold-mine known as "The Dot". Doctor Sparks, one of Townsville's earliest medical men, followed up a 'good tip' from an informer and invested a lot of money there in hopeful anticipation of making a fortune for himself and his young wife Dorothy. He named the mine after her, but all they got were lumps of quartz. Harry Butler, speaking to Jessie Macqueen about it years later, said, "Oh yes, there is gold on the Island, but not there." In reply to her further eager enquiries he only smiled quizzically. Not tor him, any more gold seekers despoiling his Island .

Inevitably though, on an Island the size of Magnetic, more settlers began to arrive, taking up land in the other bays and pioneering in their own way. Yet over the years 'Grandad' Butler, as he came to be known, remained the patriarch of the Isle. With his long silvery beard and wavy hair upon his shoulders he really looked the part. He was described as "the very kernel of Magnetic Island".

The following story was told about him in later years after Mrs Butler died and all the children had left the Island except Nell, who stayed with her father to manage a small staff at the guest house. Grandad would not miss his daily swim tor anything, in spite of Nell's continued warnings about sharks. The old man would throw off all his clothes on the beach to swim nude - but never forgetting his pipe and umbrella. With the sun-shade up and the old pipe smoking, he'd lie on his back and kick his way merrily around the Bay, floating from point to point, while Nell gazed anxiously out to sea to watch for a continuing movement from the old white head under the umbrella. When asked about sharks he replied , "Oh yes, sometimes - I saw a big fellow not far from me one day but I didn't make any fuss. I just paddled quietly to the shore, so he didn't touch me and I didn't touch him."

A sailing cutter owned by Harry Butler (junior)

Harold Butler died on 25th January, 1924 at the age of 89, his wife having passed away many years before. Most of the children left the Island to go their own ways, but a son George lived in Townsville to carry on with the Island ferry service for many years in competition with the fast developing Hayles service. As already mentioned Nell stayed on and she married a Scottish blacksmith, Will Fraser, in the first wedding ceremony held on Magnetic Island. Will Fraser suffered ill health later and died in 1940. Nell Fraser lived to a great age like her father, becoming the white-haired old Lady of the Magnetical Isle, who had spent her whole lifetime within its sanctuary. Nelly Bay was named after her. She lived to see the marvel of electricity come to the Island in 1955, then being 83 years old when she featured in a newspaper article of the day. Nell Fraser died on 19th August, 1957 aged 85 years, leaving a son William Leslie Fraser.

The 'Palm Queen', a ketch owned by Harry Butler (junior) who lived on Palm Island in the early 1900's

In the Townsville Daily Bulletin· of August 26th, 1946 an article was written on the occasion . of George Butler's 74th birthday, describing many of his experiences. George recalled taking over from his father in the early 1900's the old motor vessel Tivoli in which he carried on a good deal of private charter work. One such charter involved a prolonged nine week search in 1911 for the Adelaide Steamship Company's *Yongola,* which disappeared with 120 people aboard en route between Townsville and Mackay during a storm. George said that his brother Harry, who was an early settler on Palm Island, found a wooden cabin trunk washed ashore from the *Yongola* wreck. The trunk had been owned by a Mrs Mowbray of Charters Towers and in it were some dress lengths purchased as a present for her daughters, the name tags still on each bundle. They were duly delivered to the girls as a result of Harry's efforts. Mailbags from the same wreck were washed ashore as far away as Hinchinbrook Island. The wreck of the *Yongola* was not found until 47 years later. In September 1958 four young weekend divers from Townsville saw the still intact 300 foot long hull, covered with heavy marine growth, 90 feet under water, 12 miles off Cape Bowling Green.

In 1929 George Butler chartered the *Tivoli* to an American scientific expedition (the Yonge Expedition) to the Barrier Reef, where they spent three months in the vicinity of Low Island. Scientists later sent him many mementoes of their time together. Tivoli was eventually destroyed by fire in 1934 while George was returning alone from a trip to Dunk Island, where Hugo Brassey was erecting chalets at that time. Somewhere north of Hinchinbrook, *Tivoli's* engine back-fired and set the boat alight, but George managed to escape in the dinghy.

Harry Butler (junior), George's brother, settled on Great Palm Island about 1900 before the Aboriginal mission commenced there in 1918. The spot where he built a house for his wife and adopted son, Waiter George (who was also known as George Butler) became known as "Butler-vale" to visiting ship's crews. It was a pleasant little bay just south of the present Aboriginal settlement in Challenger Bay. Harry Butler grew a long beard like his father on Magnetic. A seaman on the A.U.S.N. coastal steamer *Palmer* in about 1912, Mr R. Bowbrick of Surrey, England, recalled in a letter to a friend in Townsville that on the regular visits by the *Palmer* to the Palm Islands, Harry would meet them in his boat, the *Palm Queen,* with a crew of two Aborigines and a black retriever dog, to exchange cargo. The steamer unloaded its consignment for the Butlers, while the cheerful Harry always offered something from the Island — a pig in a crate, a bag of oysters, or a large clam.

Weekend visitors from Townsville often went out to "Butler-vale" on Great Palm, but sometimes it was a 24 hour sail in the *Palm Queen* in light breezes — not as conveniently close as Magnetic Island. Harry's adopted son George left Palm Island in 1922 to work in 'Townsville where he married and had a daughter Georgina, who became Mrs 'Georgie' Ridge of Townsville. The property at "Butler-vale" passed to another owner for a few years after the mission started , but the lease was eventually resumed by the government.

***

In 1899 another very enterprising man came to live on Magnetic Island, to build an hotel in Picnic Bay not far from the Butler guest house. His name was Robert Hayles (senior). Born in London in 1843 he migrated to Australia at the age of 18, going first to Brisbane. He worked on sheep-stations, went gold-mining and kept a store and hotel before visiting Magnetic Island in 1898. Robert Hayles foresaw the Island's tourist potential at a time when there were plenty of people with money in the booming town of Charters Towers, just inland from the port of Townsville. He put all his money and energies into building up a business on the Island. This included the erection of a two-storied hotel and separate dance-hall in a spot not far behind the present Hotel Magnetic; a jetty of his own, some distance west of the Butler jetty; and the buying of a small steam ferry The Bee of 100 tons, brought up from Sydney where she was originally on the Sydney- Manly service.

The vision of Robert Hayles paid off, for today the company Hayles Magnetic Island Pty Ltd is a major one in the tourist industry of North Queensland. Offshoots of the parent company now operate in Cairns running a service to Green Island and Cooktown, in Canberra cruising on Lake Burley Griffin, and another service on the Brisbane River to Moreton Bay and Lone Pine.

Robert Hayles (Snr.) founder of Hayles Magnetic Island Pty Ltd

However, the road to success is never easy. In 1901, soon after he established himself in Picnic Bay, Robert Hayles' steamer *The Bee* was wrecked on Knobby Point (close to the site of the present day baths). The boat was a total loss. Unperturbed, Mr Hayles and his sons built another boat, the *Phoenix,* 32 feet long, with a 10 H.P. Hercules engine, licensed to carry 22 passengers. This he completed in 1904 but in the meantime the great cyclone "Leonta" of March 1903 had destroyed his jetty, which had to be rep laced at great cost and effort. Jetties in all the bays on the Island have, over the years, cost Hayles' thousands of dollars. Then in 1911 the Picnic Bay hotel was burnt down, to be rebuilt in 1912.

The island's popularity continued though, and soon the little *Phoenix* was unable to cope with the demand. Robert Hayles then commissioned the building of the 46 foot *Magnet* in 1906, only to find that this, too, was becoming overcrowded. A continuing line of still larger boats of the Hayles fleet followed over the years, all but a few having names beginning with the letter" M": *Magneta, Malanda, Mandalay, Maroubra, Malita, Magera, Maree, Marena, Marina, Magnetic, Majestic, Marlee, Myana, Merinda, Mirimar, Mirabel, Mirana, Mingela, Townsville, Tangalooma, Palmer, Myra* (barge); *Ferry Alma, Mimosa, Point Lookout* (vehicular-ferry) and *Minerva.*

The story of jetties on Magnetic Island is one of continuing frustration and expense. An early photograph of Picnic Bay shows no less than three jetties jutting out from the beach: one on the eastern end known as Butler's jetty, a central one on the site of the present jetty (then owned by Hayles but not the same structure) and the remains of Hayles' earlier jetty near the baths. When the Hayles company expanded operations to include Arcadia in 1914 and Nelly Bay and Horseshoe Bay soon after, there were three more jetties to be built and maintained against all odds. The first jetties at Nelly and Arcadia consisted of landings built on piles in deep water just off the rocks at Bright Point and Bremner Point respectively, connected to the mainland by long, narrow walkways. The earliest of these at Nelly Bay was without even a handrail - a rickety, four-foot wide walkway on narrow piles standing twelve feet out of the water at low tide, requiring the balance sense of a tightrope walker in a strong wind.

The *Townsville Evening Star* of Saturday, June 11th, 1927 reported that Hayles had just completed the erection of a new jetty at Arcadia costing nearly £5,000. It replaced the earlier one built for Mr Hayles by Messrs McKerracher & Murray, which had extensions made to it over the years, but which finally had to be demolished. The new structure built by Hornibrook & Co., the article reported, was most substantial and built into the side of the rocky promontory as far as possible. It was connected to the shore at Arcadia by a roadway 1400 feet long, cut into the cliffs. A stone wall eight feet wide, accommodating a set of lines for a trolley to convey goods, was included. The landing had a 66 foot frontage and 120 feet depth, and was decked with 9 inch by 3 inch timbers giving a berth of 13 foot water depth.

However, this expensive structure at Arcadia was wrecked by the 1940 cyclone, at the same time as a similar new jetty at Nelly Bay was destroyed. The Nelly Bay jetty, which also had been built closer into the rocks than the earlier 'walk-way' version, had its stone causeway washed out by the storm, leaving a group of jetty stumps, still visible today, standing off the rocks. With the advent of roads on the Island, linking Nelly to Picnic Bay, the Nelly Bay jetty was never reconstructed.

The Arcadia landing was again replaced, though not immediately after the cyclone, with a landing closer in under the lee of the Point. Its cost in 1963 was $12,000. The old 1927 landing is still standing where it was repaired in 1940, presenting the best jetty fishing near deep water on the Island.

Latest addition to the landing facilities at Arcadia is the ramp for unloading the vehicular-ferry, completed in 1967, which together with road-widening cost $6,000. Associated with this project was extensive dredging work in Arcadia Bay for the approaches to the ramp; another $12,000.

The second jetty at Arcadia, built for Hayles Magnetic in 7927 at a cost of £5,000. It is now a favourite fishing spot, having been replaced by another structure closer inshore to the right

Horseshoe Bay jetty, which was the only one not originally a Hayles construction, also suffered over the years. It has been continually renovated by the Harbours & Marine Department. The new Picnic Bay jetty completed in 1960 is another Harbours & Marine construction in association with the Townsville City Council. Other recent investments by Hayles have been the construction of a special vehicular-ferry ramp and freight loading terminal at the Townsville end, on the Banks of Ross Creek, in addition to the purchase of vehicular -ferries themselves.

Founder of the Company, Robert Hayles senior, died on 19th August, 1926, aged 82 years. He was buried in a quiet spot behind Arcadia near the grave of Dr. McCabe, one of the earliest settlers at Arcadia. Robert Hayles' sons Frank, Bob, Jack, Charles and Len carried on the business. Charles went to Cairns, Jack to Darwin (another early offshoot of the Company), Bob remained in Townsville and Frank stayed on the Island. Mr E.R. (Bob) Hayles, managing-director of the Company for many years, lived in retirement at a pleasant spot at the foot of Castle Hill, with an enviable view of the big island in Cleveland Bay which lured his father so many years ago. Another generation of Hayles boys have now taken over operation of the firm.

Hayles' passenger-ferry service is now indispensible to life on the Island, and the company has played a major part in the Magnetic Island story. We will have more to say about the sturdy boats which carry on day after day, year after year, even close in the wake of a cyclone.

Hayles ferry leaving Picnic Bay jetty

The original thatched, Japanese style, Mandalay guest house, erected in Nelly Bay by Mrs. Brand (using Japanese workers) in 1912

CHAPTER 4
MORE PIONEERS

An interesting early description of the Isle comes from the pen of E. J. Banfield, the 'Beachcomber' of Dunk Island in the early 1900's. Banfield of course became famous for his book *The Confessions of a Beachcomber*, describing his life on Dunk.

Banfield was a professional journalist, at one time co-editor of the *Townsville Daily Bulletin* newspaper, but became so ill and exhausted from overwork and as he put it, "the poisonous years of the past" (civilisation), that his doctor pronounced it unlikely he would live more than six months if he continued the way he was going. He was forty-five, when in 1897 he settled on Dunk Island with his wife Bertha to build himself a bungalow, cultivate fruit, keep cows and goats and catch fish from the shores of his island. He lived to the age of 71 and during his 25 years of island life, wrote numerous articles ('Rural Homilies' was a regular feature in the *Townsville Bulletin*) and four books, among which was *The Confessions*. Other writings of Banfield's included a handbook he compiled in 1907, called *Within the Barrier — Tourist's Guide to the North Queensland Coast*. His reference to Magnetic Island was as follows:

> "Magnetic Island atones for some of the barrenness and aridity of the mainland opposite. Spots may be selected there where the refreshment and free growth of climates blessed with a far more bountiful rainfall may be obtained, for a considerable area of the surface of the island is an elevated plateau, rough, rugged and seamed, but which holds the rain for a season, allowing the drainage to permeate gradually to the lower levels, filling the wells of the islanders with pure cold water, and maintaining the verdure of the valleys when the adjacent hills are withered, brown and parched."

Yet another of Banfield's publications, "Townsville illustrated", published jointly with G. H. Pritchard in December 1906, refers to Magnetic:

> "Bathing, boating, fishing, and scaling the pine-clad headlands, hunting wild goats among the hollows and basins of the hills which form the backbone of the Island. … Nellie Bay, with Bright's at the eastern corner, where is the most fruitful corner of the Island … Some day, no doubt, a great line-fishing industry will be established, tor the harvest of the sea is perennial, plentiful and richly varied. Hitherto climatic conditions have interposed and frown upon the success of the trade, but the employment of speedy oil-launches and abundance of ice must brush aside all these disadvantages. This art and industry of

> deep-sea fishing among the wonders of the Great Barrier Reef will have Magnetic tor its base."

Bantield's prophesy about a fishing industry has not yet really come true, but there arc a few professional fishermen based in Horseshoe Bay, with 'speedy oil -launches', and deep-freeze units with a capacity undreamed of in the days of ice. We note also that goats then roamed the Island, another depredator of vegetation almost as bad as fire. Thankfully, there are none left now.

A contemporary of Banfield's was Dodd S. Clarke, Editor of the *Townsville Bulletin* from 1881 until 1915. Clarke had his first look at the north while on a visit to his uncle, police magistrate at Cardwell in the late 70's. Clarke's first venture in journalism was the publication of a newspaper at Cairns in partnership with J. K. Mehan. Then with a third partner Rhodes, he went to Townsville in 1881 to found the *Townsville Daily Bulletin*, which he ran for 34 years. Dodd Clarke was living at 'Our Is land Home' in Nelly Bay (the red-roofed cottage which became better known as a tea-room and guest-house run by Mrs Tidey, and later owned by Graham and Jo Wieneke) as early as 1890, and stayed there until his death on July 10th, 1918. A writer of a later period had this to say about the man:

> "The restful atmosphere of Magnetic Island gives much happiness to its residents, and encourages the studious to write in philosophical strain like Mr Banfield did at Dunk Island. I refer particularly to Mr Dodd S. Clarke, most of whose writings were penned at Nelly Bay."

***

The Magnetic Island coastline was surveyed by J. G. O'Connell in 1886, many of the bays being named after the children of the

Pearce family then living in Townsville — Arthur, Florence, Alma, Geoffrey and Nellie. The latter name,-Nellie, may have been mere coincidence, for as we have already seen, Jessie Macqueen was sure Nelly Bay was named after Nell Butler. Another story circulates that "Nellie" was an old black gin living in that bay for many years. A "Baldwin Bay", ostensibly named after Mrs Pearce's maiden name, was also listed by O'Connell. However there is no such bay on present maps, though it could have been corrupted to "Balding", which is the beautiful little beach adjacent to Radical Bay on the north-eastern corner of the Isle. *Radical* was the name of the survey vessel.

The first settlers to follow the Butlers on the Island were Mr and Mrs Well beloved, who came from South Africa to try their luck in Horseshoe Bay. They made a gallant attempt for a couple of years to raise pigs and grow fruit and vegetables for a living , including the planting of a vineyard which was a total failure. They spent over £3,000 on the venture, but inexperience in the ways of the land, combined with ill health, proved too much for them in the end, forcing them to return to the mainland, though not before they had the first white child to be born on the Isle — Nita Wellbeloved.

It was left to more experienced farmers like the Apjohns, Swenson, Neilsen, Parker, Bolger, Anderson, Van der Blich, and Hughes brothers, to put Horseshoe Bay on the map with its eventual big export of delicious pineapples. Lloyd Apjohn and his two sons started pineapple farming in Horseshoe Bay in 1913. One son, George, carried on growing 'pines' successfully for over twenty years before selling out to retire in Toowoomba. George Apjohn was well known for his feats of sheer strength and stamina, common among many pioneer Australians. He was a giant of a man. A typical performance would be on a day he met the launch at Arcadia. No roads then — George Apjohn would carry two heavy sacks of pineapples on his shoulders, walking the four miles over steep ridges following the goat track between Horseshoe Bay and Arcadia. Then, after delivering his load, he would pick up two rolls of heavy-gauge fencing wire, crossing them over his head and shoulders, before taking up an additional two sacks of food to plod all the way home. George was not only a hard worker; he was a deep thinker and a good conversationalist too — a real character.

Harry Lindberg, with his wife and five children, was among the earliest of the old-timers at Horseshoe Bay, his specialty being boatbuilding. The sailing vessels, all cutters — the *Goldfinch, Boomerang, Trueblue* and *Isa* — were his creations, built in Horseshoe Bay.

The first 'would-be' farmers in Nelly Bay were an unnamed trio, described by Grandad Butler as complete no-hopers. "Couldn't even grow a blade of grass and never tried," he said. They were a married couple and a single man, partners in an attempt to grow fruit and vegetables. All they could do, according to Grandad, was to fight among themselves, until in the end the married man tired of the whole affair and his wife included. He sold his wife to the other man for a sack of potatoes and quit the Island; or so insisted Grandad in story-telling mood.

Other early settlers to try cultivation in Nelly Bay were Messrs Vestergaard and Petersen, followed by Joe Butler, a brother of Harry's. However, William Bright became the most successful in this Bay. He built a house near the present school, with timber obtained mainly from a shipwreck, the *Seattle* in 1901. With his wife and daughter he grew pineapples, pawpaws and mangoes, the last being used to brew a beverage, mango wine, for which he became well known by visiting sailing boat crews. They reckoned Bright's wine had a real kick in it. Bright Point is named after him.

Otto Bottiger's house at Nelly Bay, 1918

A man who went to Nelly Bay about the same time as Dodd S. Clarke in 1890 was Otto Bottiger, who was still there in 1931, according to Mr Mcllwaine's broadcast already referred to Jessie Macqueen also mentions him, saying that no one seemed to know where he came from, but that it was obvious he was a learned man. The sturdy, black-bearded Bottiger cared little for his personal appearance, says Miss Macqueen, yet he could quote Shakespeare from beginning to end, and would recite classical poems to any good listener for as long as they dared stay. ''He was always unkempt," she said, "yet the man still possessed those unmistakable signs which go hand in hand with distinguished bearing and high breeding. What possessed him to live the life of a nomad no one ever knew." His dwelling was every bit as odd as the man; an untidily contrived structure of timber and thatch, built on four wooden piles out on the edge of the sand-bar a hundred yards or so along the beach from the old rambling walkway of the original Nelly Bay jetty, completely surrounded by sea water at high tide. His front door opened to the sea, the back door leading on to the shore. Jessie Macqueen reckoned it resembled, from a distance, a big ship's funnel, salvaged from some wreck and just dumped in shallow water.

When the first school on the Island commenced operations in Picnic Bay, Mr Bottiger was included as a member of the school committee because of his wide education. Children walked to this school from every bay on the Island before Nelly and Horseshoe organised their own schools. However, when it came to committee meetings, Otto Bottiger remained as informal as ever. A prominent lady of the Picnic Bay fraternity, Mrs Eyre, is quoted as saying indignantly after one such meeting, "He arrived late of course, but worse than that he was unshaven, coatless, hatless, shoeless, and a pair of frightful looking trousers rolled up to the knees. The worst of it was," sighed Mrs Eyre, "no one dared say a word of protest to him."

In 1924 when Nelly Bay organised its own provisional school, conducted in the old kiosk building of "Mandalay" guest house, Otto Bottiger was again prominent in its affairs. His name is remembered on a wrought iron "Bottiger Memorial" entrance archway to the school tennis court at Nelly Bay, which has only recently been removed to another position to make way for new building extensions. Bottiger also conducted the Nelly Bay post-office for many years, and Mr McIlwaine said of him in 1931, "If you care for real good fish yarns, all true, of course, I recommend you to spend an hour or two in the company of Mr Otto Bottiger. Our old friend Jonah, he of the whale episode, has nothing over "old Bot" when fish stories are to be told."

Apart from "Our Island Home" guest house, which was built under the lee of Bright Point at the end of the old Nelly

Bay jetty walkway, in one of the most pleasant sites on the Island, and run by Mrs Tidey for years, tourists in Nelly Bay were also catered for by "Mandalay" guest house. In 1912 Mrs Brand spent over £6,000 in developing this picturesque resort in an area just back from the beach opposite the Nelly Bay store. Some of the thirteen odd-shaped little cottages with high-peaked roofs are still standing in various properties of the now completely sub-divided block. The little huts may look strange today with their peaked galvanized iron roofing, but the original concept was for an entirely thatched roof rustic setting, including the big central dining-room. Mrs Brand brought in Japanese craftsman to do all the artistic thatching in Japanese style, and early photographs indicate that they did achieve a quite pleasing effect, especially regarding the main building. For one thing, it was very much cooler than the subsequent iron roofing which replaced the thatch when the latter rotted. However, the place was not very well patronized — Mrs Brand was a little ahead of her time, and there were just not enough tourists to go round between all the places mushrooming on the Island during those years. She had lost a lot of money by the time she sold Mandalay to Jack O'Leary in 1922. The place rapidly became rundown; not at all like the original rustic Island resort Mrs Brand had envisaged. Mrs Dempster took it over in December 1926 to give it a new lease of life for a while. Her husband, a carpenter, who built many of the substantial earlier homes on the Island, completely rebuilt all the roofs with galvanized iron; a safer and more permanent covering even if less appealing aesthetically. But" Mandalay" drifted into obscurity soon after the township of Nelly Bay was surveyed and sub-divided into smaller allotments for private homes.

Before the turn of the century, Arcadia was first settled by Captain Petersen and two fishermen friends, Nicholas Monti and Zurich, who built a cottage under the trees on the beach-front. Captain Petersen spent his holidays there between his sea-going voyages, but their buildings and boats were eventually washed out in a combination of rough seas and high tides, causing them to shift camp to Cockle Bay, where Nicholas Monti stayed to become well known in that part — he died there in 1928.

A Frenchman, Edward Armand, then came to Arcadia to have it properly surveyed, and applied for a lease of the whole grounds which comprise the present establishment of Arcadia Hotel. Mr and Mrs Armand and their son had log cabins built with thatched roofing, and laid out the extensive garden grounds with coconut palms, tamarinds and various fruit trees, to make a pleasant 'Arcadian' setting for visitors from the mainland. With their 22 foot sailing boat, the *Duke,* skippered by a Russian Finn, Tom Skinnery, the Armands brought over many guests to holiday at what became known as " Frenchman's Bay".

In 1906 the Armands sold to Dr McCabe, a dentist from Townsville, who retained it for his own use — a place where he entertained friends brought over in his yacht the *Viking*. He died there and is buried at Arcadia. Next in succession to this property were Mr and Mrs L. Rheuben who again ran Arcadia as a guest house, until it was sold to the Hayles family in 1914. For many years Mr C. C. D. (Sandy) Laver, a Director of Hayles Magnetic Company, and his wife Ethel, a granddaughter of Robert Hayles senior, ran the completely rebuilt Arcadia Hotel in its still attractive garden landscape setting, close to both Geoffrey Bay and Alma Bay beaches.

Reverting back to Picnic Bay of the early 1900's: the Eyre family were managing Hayles' hotel and later running the post-office. Mr Eyre, a surveyor, died some years before his widow, who became well known in the Bay for her energetic support of Island progress committees and school welfare etc. Jessie Macqueen tells a story of Mrs Eyre and Grandad Butler's favourite pet bull. One day while walking home through the bush, Mrs Eyre became the centre of attention for the young bull, which suddenly chased her full-pelt through the trees. She ran terrified, barely managing to roll lengthways under the bottom barbed wire of a paddock fence adjoining her property, before 'bully' snorted at the fence. Mrs Eyre complained bitterly to everyone about that animal, but Grandad had his defence at the ready. He explained lightheartedly, "That little bull — he never chased Mrs Eyre at all. What he wanted her to do, was to scratch his head between the horns, same as I always do when I meet him in the bush. But Mrs Eyre of course, she started running and the bull he was only running to see what Mrs Eyre was running for."

***

The story of early settlement on the Island is not complete until one has penetrated into the lovely beaches around its north-eastern corner. These relatively unspoiled bays are the least seen, being off the beaten track — Arthur, Florence, Radical and Balding. Arthur Bay can be reached from the main road between Arcadia and Horseshoe Bay along a track descending through a pleasant, lightly timbered valley with denser pockets of Hoop-pine forest at its lower end. A cottage stands close to the beach here on a private lease taken up in the 1920's by Elliott Markwick, of whom we will have more to say.

Clem Ladbury, 37 years in Radical Bay

From the northern end of Arthur Bay the track continues across a low peninsula to Florence Bay, site of the present-day Boy Scout camp. The beach here is a broad strip of white sand, not quite so steeply shelving as Arthur, with a line of weeping Sheoak trees along the foreshore. Groves of aged coconut palms at both ends of the bay, together with a group of huts in the southern corner, bear witness to earlier times in this secluded spot, with its extensive area of flat hinterland between the beach and the steep granite ridges climbing to the war-time Fort establishment above.

Florence Bay from the Fort

The lease of 38 acres at Florence Bay was first taken up in November 1915 by Asher Morris Benjamin from Charters Towers, who built a small guest house and spent £600 on a jetty which was eventually washed away. No trace of the latter remains today, but one of the original huts is used by the scouts. Mr Benjamin brought in much of his materials by horse-back from Horseshoe Bay as well as by sea, aided in the former by George Apjohn with his team of horses. Horses were also used to pull in jetty piles. But it was all to no avail for the project fell through before it really got under way. Harry Butler's son George deposited the first load of guests by boat one Easter weekend. Florence Bay is wide open to a sou'easter and when heavy weather prevented George from returning in his boat from Picnic Bay to pick up the guests at the end of their stay, they all had to walk out through the bush carrying their belongings. The incident was enough to discourage any more Florence Bay holiday-makers.

Not until the second World War did Florence Bay hum again to the sound of many voices — those not too unfortunate soldiers and sailors who were posted to the Fort Battery overlooking the enticing beach below. Two of the present scout huts were constructed at that time as a recreation base for the servicemen. After the war a keen Boy Scout leader, Louis Varsey Masters (known as "Beaver"), took a closer look at the deserted beach from his shack at nearby Radical Bay, where he lived on and off from 194 7. With the aid of donating patrons including Sir Leslie Wilson and Bob Hayles, Beaver Masters founded the Sir Leslie Wilson Scout Camp in August 1956, taking up the lease of the whole bay, and buying buildings on the site from the government. The locale was idyllic for scout camps — shower-heads rigged up among the granite boulders for a natural 'bathroom' — a quiet open-air chapel in a bush clearing — flag-pole and ceremonial ground in another spot, and shady trails criss-crossing through the bush to the creek and the beach. Beaver Masters died on 15th May, 1964 and his ashes now rest on a memorial plaque erected at the chapel, showing the familiar 'circle-dot' insignia in scout language for 'gone home'.

The track from the Fort down through Florence Bay passes out over the northern peninsula to Radical Bay, a place well timbered with shady trees around the modern cabins of a secluded tourist resort known as 'Magnetic Haven'. A very early lease of 4 acres at Radical was taken out in 1915 by William Fraser, husband of Nellie Butler, but he relinquished it in 1917 without developing the site. Again, in 1917 another portion of 4 acres was leased by four people — Messrs Grant, Leone, Lear and Johns, but also surrendered in 1919.

Radical Bay (foreground) and Balding Bay

Radical was first settled in 1922 when Elliott Chalmers Markwick built a cottage at the eastern end of the bay, later owned by Clem Ladbury, who supplied most of the information for this story of the 'north-east corner'. Clem said that Mr Markwick was a partner with his father in the western Queensland firm of Ladbury & Co., operating at Carrar (near Richmond) and Talmoi (near Maxwellton) in the shearing, woolclassing and wool-scouring business. Elliott Markwick took to visiting Magnetic Island during off-seasons, staying at Arcadia and Florence Bay guest house while the latter was still operating. He retired in 1922 with the idea of living on the Island, seeking firstly a lease of Arthur Bay as previously mentioned. However, the Lands Department suggested Radical Bay as a wiser choice because it offered more shelter from the weather than the sou'easterly exposed Arthur Bay. He leased the whole of Radical, and with his sister lived out his life there, catching fish and smoking them for his own use and growing vegetables and fruit. Miss Markwick died in 1936 at the age of eighty, not long after Clem Ladbury first came to live at Radical.

Clem Ladbury drifted for a few years, going as far as Papua New Guinea before returning to Radical in 1937. When Elliott Markwick passed away in 1945 aged eighty, followed by another friend, Charles Coar, who at one time lived on Orpheus Island before shifting to Radical Bay, Clem Ladbury was left on his own in the peaceable surroundings with the Currawongs and Butcher-birds and wailing Bush-curlews his only company.

In those days the regular ferry service ran as far as Horseshoe Bay, calling at Radical each Tuesday to deliver bread, meat and mail. It was 1947 when Beaver Masters took up residence nearby, followed by G.F. Leitch, an artist, in 1950, but these men too passed on, leaving Clem again sole resident of the bay. Clem's seclusion came to an end in 1960 when Bob Wake embarked on his 'cabins in the wilderness' scheme for a tourist resort, and Clem eventually married and shifted to Horseshoe Bay.

Balding Bay, adjoining Radical, nestles into the coastline just past a rocky headland known as Fish-hawk Rock, famous for its large stick nest of an Osprey or White-headed Fish-hawk. Balding is the only one of the four north-eastern beaches which has retained its virginity. The Osprey's nest has stood undisturbed for many years, and one hopes that the pure sands of Balding Bay will remain un-disfigured with any of man's structures.

***

Bill Laurie of Townsville, retired professional photographer who first visited the Island in 1912, related the following anecdote (with a photograph to prove it) concerning longevity on Magnetic Island. In Radical Bay, he said, there is a rock which when viewed from seawards gives a distinct impression of the 'Spirit of the Isle' — the figure of a woman unmistakably outlined in markings on the rock face, with Old Father Time hovering in the background, frustrated after he came to collect the woman for another entry to his Doomsday Book, but found her instead to be alive and well. And it is a fact that many of the older generation are still hale and hearty on the Island after virtually a lifetime spent with in its health-sustaining sanctuary.

Bill Laurie photographed the whole Island over the years, recording its various phases of development and capturing many of its picturesque aspects to print on post cards for sale to tourists. Among these were early photographs of Mandalay Guest House and Our Island Home in Nelly Bay. Also 'The Retreat' in Horseshoe Bay, and a series of comical postcards taken in the 1930's depicting various 'rockpaintings' (which today would be considered graffiti) around the Island.

Another long-lived couple on the Island, Harry Rouse and his wife, came to Picnic Bay in 1925 to take over management of Hayles' Hotel. Harry Rouse knew Jessie Macqueen in Townsville as early as 1912. He was twelve years in the hotel before taking over a shop at Picnic Bay about 1937. Then in 1940 he bought the old Butler guest house from Nell Fraser, renaming it "Dunoon" after the town in Scotland where his wife was born.

An interesting job Harry Rouse recalled was rebuilding and extending a tiny church in the Bay in 1941. St. Andrews Church of England in Picnic Street must surely have been one of the smallest houses of worship ever to seat a congregation. Before it was extended by two feet on either side, it was a mere 20 feet by 12 feet. It had been put there sometime in the 1930's when it was removed from its original position in Nelly Bay next to the Mandalay Guest House, where it served as the first Nelly Bay State School.

The western coastline of Magnetic has been, and still is, relatively unpopulated. Mangrove swamps and a rough bush track have kept it almost as quiet as it was when the Aborigines had their last camp in Ned Lee's Creek. A few others followed Nicolas Monti at Cockle Bay, including the Olsens who settled there in the early 1900's to engage in fishing.

Apart from the Bolgers of Bolger's Bay, and the Grays who ran a guest house at West Point not far from the old quarantine station (George Gray was one-time world billiards champion) there have been only one or two other small farms along that track. The West Point guest house became overrun by white-ants within a few years, and is now a ruin.

A well known family in Nelly Bay, the Colemans, settled in the Gustav Valley against the foothills of Mount Cook. Octavius Coleman, an Englishman, went first with his wife and family to Arcadia in 1931, growing citrus trees and pawpaws before shifting to the larger property at Nelly Bay in 1949. His son Steve (senior), then recently back from war service in Papua New Guinea, also took on farming pineapples on an adjoining property. Steve and wife Christine built a pleasant cottage on the banks of Gustav Creek in the cool shade of the jungle beneath a ridge leading to Mount Cook. This area, during the Wet Season immediately after rain, is a myriad of glistening waterfalls cascading over rockfaces on the steep ridges, with the roar of rapids over stony creek beds all around.

Mrs Coleman senior's rainfall record, dating from 1944, gives the Island's average as about 60 inches (1520 mm) per annum, compared to Townsville's 47 .3 inches over the same period. The official figure over a much longer period (100 years) in Townsville is 43.06 inches (1 090 mm). The wettest year on record for the Island was 1950, when 110.78 inches fell. Townsville's total for that year was 86.40 inches. The individual monthly figures of Mrs Coleman's record indicate that Magnetic Island receives much more benefit from the mid-year rains in June and July than does the mainland. Being 8 kilometres offshore, the Island seems more favourably located for the seasonal south-east winds, and temperatures on the Island are generally a few degrees lower than in Townsville.

Adjoining Steve Coleman's farm in Nelly Bay, nearer the head of Gustav Creek, is a 14 acre property first settled in 1918 by a 32 year old man from Cardwell, Herbert Douglas. The land was then valued at 10 4/5 pence per acre. Herbert Douglas cleared timber and established pineapples, pawpaws and citrus trees before relinquishing the block in 1921. It changed hands three more times before a more permanent settler, Patrick John Walsh, bought it on 15th January, 1931. 'Paddy' Walsh is well remembered as a genuine bushman from western Queensland. He cleared more bush, sank another well 35 feet deep in a position higher up the slopes, where only one who really knew about water would risk striking an underground stream, and made a comfortable living growing 'pines', pawpaws, bananas and citrus. Paddy retired to the Eventide Home at Charters Towers in 1952. This same property later became my own home for a few years.

There are other, long since departed pioneers, whose stories will only ever be vaguely remembered. Tom Farrell, who conducted the Nelly Bay post office for many years from his home in Barton Street, came to the Island from western Queensland in the late 20's.

A hardy woman pioneer, Miss Ivy Kennedy, ran a pineapple and dairy farm unaided in Nelly Bay before the war. She took her pineapples down to Hayles' launch on a horse-drawn sled. Miss Kennedy called all her cows by individual names at milking time, only the particular animal called coming up for its turn. When one of her pets lay dying with bloat in the paddock one day, the distressed woman, through her tears, put a slit in the cow's stomach to try and save it, but it died.

Jack Morley, the frail little man of Upper Mandalay Avenue, who ran a pineapple farm where now stands the Mediterranean Village resort, led an adventurous life before he came to the Island. He left England in 1922 to spend six months in north-western Queensland, before going to Fiji to join the C.S.R. Company for two or three years. While in Fiji he heard of the rubber boom in Malaya and followed his itchy feet there in 1925 to take a job as assistant manager on a plantation. He returned to England in 1930, but before the end of 1931 Jack Morley was back in Australia again, humping a swag through the Kimberleys in the Northwest looking for gold with two mates. They found none, and when one of his friends got into trouble with the police at Derby, Jack dreamt again of the Pacific Islands. With his brother, Jack took up a copra plantation on Tovu-lai-lai Island in the Fiji group in 1933.

The plantation failed and Jack left his brother in Fiji to return to Malaya for the second time to work on another rubber plantation in the heart of the jungle. Big game hunting was a spare time occupation at that time, but the Japanese were already building up for their even bigger hunting game over the following years. Jack was still in Malaya when the Japs landed on the northeast coast of the peninsula and was taken prisoner-of-war. For the rest of the war he worked on the Burma-Siam railway — a period of near starvation and brutality which permanently affected his health. He was repatriated to England in 1945, but two years back there in the cold, damp clime of the Old Country was more than he could stand. Though his doctor advised against a return to the tropics, Jack Morley did go back to Malaya in 1947, unfortunately just at the time many of his old plantation friends were murdered by Communist terrorists. He left Malaya for the last time in 1948 bound for the Great Barrier Reef coastline, and eventually to the serenity of an old pineapple farm on the Magnetical Island.

***

The late Martin Carlson, the 'quiet philosopher' of Fish Cove near Arcadia, could tell many an interesting yarn of the early days on Magnetic. Martin was an ardent conservationist in the days well before there was any real public awareness of the need to protect our natural environment. As honorary Forest Ranger on Magnetic Island for many years, he showed conscientious concern for the welfare of flora and fauna in the National Park. He was an early climber to the summit of Mount Cook, and walked over the whole Island which he knew like the back of his hand. Well on, in his later years, he still found fascination in the old granite Isle which he continued to explore actively, strolling around to little known corners in the various bays, keeping an eye on things.

An impressively tall figure, Martin Carlson first arrived in North Queensland in 1916 as a seaman from Sweden, took a liking to the tropical climate and stayed. His early visits to the Island during the 1920's prompted him to construct a cottage at Fish Cove which he first used as a weekender, but which from 1942 became his permanent home. A name plate, "Journey's End", guided one to his quiet sanctuary on the cliffs overlooking Cleveland Bay and the rocky cove below. He welcomed callers, and many were the interesting personalities who left their names in the visitor's book kept by his housekeeper, Mrs Valentine.

Martin Carlson of Fish Cove, 1969

Martin's wide ranging interests took in especially the many fields of natural history. During one of our conversations together on his front verandah looking out over the cove, he mentioned that dugong were once plentiful around the Island. Before shark nets were set up to protect swimming beaches, he said he used to watch mother dugong suckling their young and swimming in the clear water — a wonderful sight, the young following every movement of the mother as though attached by an unseen cord, while they dived into the depths. Now they have disappeared, and one can only assume that meshing has been responsible, for harmless dugong were often taken in the shark nets and injured beyond recovery. The few which did escape, instinctively steered clear in future — so Magnetic Island is that much poorer because of the fairly slight risk of shark attack.

Martin had very strong ideas on all aspects of conservation. On such a relatively dry island, fire, he said, is one of the biggest threats, yet people just will not take it seriously enough. So long as their houses and property are not touched, little thought is given to a blaze in the bush, but the vegetation of the Island has suffered acutely from repeated conflagrations allowed to run riot. He described how grass fires lit through the timber each year, apart from destroying seedlings, damage the lower trunks of older trees where the bark is scorched, especially of trees like the Hoop pine which was once prolific over the Island. Each year more of the bark is destroyed, then fire eats into the exposed raw timber, eventually creating a hollow on the windward side which in the end will ignite the whole tree and kill it. He said he saw the same thing in the Whitsunday Islands farther south, during his seaman days. He remembered seeing islands like Dent and South Molle covered with dense stands of Hoop pine before settlers took up sheep-grazing leases on them . The settlers lit grass fires every year, and Martin said that when he sailed past in later years the beautiful pine forests had become blackened sticks.

Martin Carlson happened to witness at first hand one of the original resettlement moves of Aborigines from Mission Beach, near Tully, to the Great Palm Island Aboriginal Reserve in 1918. In that year two great cyclones visited the coast of

North Oueensland — one in January which swiped Mackay farther south, and the other near Dunk Island on 10th March, described in detail by E. J. Banfield in his posthumously published book *Last Leaves from Dunk Island.* The Dunk Island blow, which came to be known locally as the 'Innisfail cyclone' (because the eye of it passed right through .that town), did great damage along the coast, completely stripping the rain-forest for miles and causing much loss of life as well as wrecking houses and boats. Its effect was so devastating, in fact, that Aborigines living at or near the old Mission station on the mainland opposite Dunk Island were deprived of their usual food supplies. Fever broke out in their camps and many died before Banfield arranged to shift them across to camps on the sandspit at Brammo Bay on Dunk. Dunk Island itself, although badly hit, was still able to support life and was free of disease. The government finally took a hand and decided to settle the Aborigines on Palm Island. All able-bodied men were first transported to Great Palm on an old sailing vessel owned by a Townsville timber merchant. This initial contingent set to and built temporary living quarters for the gins and piccaninnies who were to follow later. In July of 1918, Martin Carlson was serving in a small steamer run by Broadfoot's of Townsville, which was chartered by the government to pick up all the remaining members of the tribe from Dunk and take them to the Palms. He recalled it was a beautiful, calm, moonlit night for the voyage, during which the crew were entertained with a wild corroboree and sing-sing over the hatchways. They arrived at Challenger Bay on Palm at 1.30am, to be rowed ashore in small dinghies.

Martin told me of another interesting phase of Magnetic Island's history during World War 11. It was then that what became known as "The Fort" was built on a hill overlooking the most attractive corner of the Island, the north-eastern sector. It was said that the island -hopping course of the invading Japanese during the early days of the war was heading them straight towards Magnetic Island and Townsville. The Magnetic Battery fortifications were installed in 1942 with the idea of protecting the main shipping entrance to Townsville Harbour, Platypus Channel, which is a dredged channel through the relatively shallow waters between a point off Magnetic Island and the rock breakwater-enclosed artificial harbour at the entrance to Ross Creek, Townsville. Magnetic's hills command a wide view of the whole of Cleveland Bay, which was then a strategic natural anchorage for allied shipping convoys, assembling for action further north. With up to forty ships in the Bay at a time, Townsville would have been a real prize to the Japanese.

One of the main functions of the Fort, known officially as the Port War Signal Station complex, was the Naval communications centre situated in a concrete block-house at the highest point on the hills, to keep meticulous watch on all shipping and aircraft in the vicinity and report back by telephone lines to other units on the Island and by radio to units on the mainland at Cape Pallarenda and Kissing Point. Two 155 mm guns were mounted on the slopes just below the signal station, operated in association with two searchlight batteries, one on the peninsula above Florence Bay half a mile to the east, the other way out on the point from White Lady Beach, two miles north. Another

The Fort, looking towards Cape Cleveland on the horizon

Radar unit operated from the most north-easterly point on the Island — a high knoll above Radical Bay, where the foundations of concrete and supporting squares of timber still exist undisturbed in the quiet bush at a spot giving a striking view of Radical and Balding Bays, with their clean white beaches below. What was not so obvious about this whole defence system was that Platypus Channel itself was mined with a series of ground-mines controlled from a pill-box at the Harbour entrance. If an enemy ship actually got as far as the channel it was to be blown up, thereby effectively blocking the entrance.

Gun emplacement near the Fort

On an island full of natural granite rock outcrops, the concrete blockhouses, well camouflaged with rounded, cement plaster facia slabs cast on iron-mesh in rock-like forms, blended in quite harmoniously with the rugged scenery. So much so, that today as a tourist attraction they do not seem at all out of place, jutting out of the hillsides amid Hoop pine forest and bush. From seawards, the quiet beaches and rocky headlands still appear much as they must have to Captain Cook.

A narrow vehicle track, constructed with great difficulty by the Queensland Main Roads Department, under instructions from the Defence Department, was the only means of access to the area. Heavy rain during the wet season played havoc with its steep grades, cut in precariously over rough ridges and awkward gullies . At that time, even the road between Arcadia and Horseshoe Bay was a mere bush track. From the highest point on this track in the Arcadia saddle, a suitable route was surveyed through thick scrub and steep hillsides leading to the chosen high vantage point for observation posts and heavy gun emplacements. The road was extended right through from Arcadia Saddle down the steep descent to Florence Bay beach, to enable them to haul up the big guns from a landing there. Some equipment slid down the hillsides before the job was completed in late 1942.

Dozens of camouflaged Army huts and tents were erected in the bush all around the area, though of these, only concrete foundations remain today, most of them already covered with rotting leaves and vegetation. Two 10,000 gallon .water tanks, fed by a two-inch pipe line along the ridges from a bore at Swenson's old farm, near the present Horseshoe Bay guest house, supplied the 140 odd Army and Navy personnel here. The guns were manned by an Australian Coastal Artillery Unit of about 100 men. Many people were under the impression that the Americans, who did so much else for Australia, were connected with this particular area. However, they did not have any control over the Fort War stat ion, being based at their own West Point Radar Unit.

The highest construction on the main ridge, a big block-house with narrow observation slits, was the nerve-centre for the whole complex, operated by the Australian Navy. From here, communication lines were laid to every point in the bush from White Lady to Florence Bay and back to Arcadia.

The guns on Magnetic Island came too late to be used in enemy action, though a few practice shots were fired out into Cleveland Bay, and there is the story that a Yank PT boat which did not answer a challenge had a shot fired across her bows. But Martin Carlson recalled watching the first Japanese air-raid on the city of Townsville before this, in early 1942, from the front verandah of his home at Fish Cove. There were only one or two other raids on Townsville during the remaining years of the war, so Jap intelligence must have been well informed of the bristling armament adorning the deceptively quiet, bush-clad hills of the big island offshore from Australia's tropic coast, which came so close to foreign invasion.

CHAPTER 5
CYCLONES AND SHIPWRECKS

The first recorded cyclone in the Townsville area occurred on 3rd March, 1867, three years after the settlement was founded, when the barometer went down to 28.246 inches. Another two less violent storms occurred in 1870 and 1890, before the monster "Sigma" of January 26th, 1896, bore down on the port. This one was followed by another full cyclone "Leonta" on March 9th, 1903. A 'severe storm' in 1927 did some damage, and there was a serious blow again on Sunday, February 18th, 1940, the unnamed '1940 cyclone'. Full blown cyclones dropped in on the coast both north and south of Townsville over the next thirty-one years without affecting the area, until the most vicious lady of them all suddenly appeared on the scene. Cyclone "Althea" came screaming in on the morning of Christmas Eve 1971 with winds of up to 140 miles per hour, her awe-inspiring 'eye' passing only ten miles to the north of Magnetic Island.

Before describing these cyclones in detail, we should first present a picture of the Port of Townsville in earlier times. The hand of man has been very busy around the waterfront since the construction of a small wharf am id the mangroves of Ross Creek in 1864. Large ships could not enter in those days; they anchored in Cleveland Bay just off Hawkings Point on Magnetic Island about five miles from the shore. Freight was transported ashore by lighters fording a sand-bar at the mouth of Ross Creek — when tides and weather permitted, that is. If a boisterous sou'easter blew up, vessels would be obliged to anchor at the western end of Magnetic Island in what became known as the 'Northern Anchorage', opposite the quarantine station on West Point. The lighters then had to travel about eight miles to shore.

The first breakwater was a rough wall of rubble and mangrove timbers on the western bank of Ross Creek (not to be confused with the mouth of the Ross River a mile further east), built in 1873 to create a scour to keep the entrance clear. The eastern breakwater was an extension from Magazine 'Island' (then connected with the mainland by a causeway), begun in 1876 and completed in 1880. Magazine Island has now become swallowed up in land reclamation on the harbour front. The western breakwater, now 5,400 feet long, was not completed until 1891, as the other side was considered sufficient protection for many years. Both breakwaters suffered severe damage in the cyclone "Sigma" and had to be restored at great cost. The repair work must have been substantial for they have withstood all tests since.

Platypus Channel, named after the dredge *Platypus* which was especially designed and built for this harbour, was begun on 5th November, 1884. The channel was dredged from the fifteen foot contour of Cleveland Bay and completed in about the year 1900. Another dredge vessel, the *Townsville,* now operates continuously over this channel, keeping it to a minimum depth of seventeen feet, the spoil being used for further land reclamation works. In operation the spoil is retained in big tanks on the ship, which settles down very noticeably in the water after a 'run'; then when she gets ashore the liquid sand is pumped out of the holds and directed through big movable pipes to the area being reclaimed.

But to return to cyclones. Cyclone "Sigma" was notable for its prolonged ferocity, hanging on as it did for three days from 26th January to the 29th, and causing immense havoc among shipping then in harbour. No less than thirty-six vessels were affected, nine of which were sunk, twelve washed up high and dry on the rocks, some with their backs broken, and fifteen others damaged. It was an in credible story of huge ships being buffeted around in side the breakwater walls, shuttling back and forth between one side and the other as the wind changed direction, causing them to break anchorage and collide with each other on the way. Even those which were able to hold anchor sustained damage from other drifting ships, such as the *Albatross,* a government steamer just arrived from Thursday Island, which put out two anchors in Harbour and got full steam-up to ride out the full force of the gale. She was slightly damaged by the colliding Presto and *Heather Bell.* Presto finished up sinking with 350 tons of coal, 9 tons of sugar and 15 tons of general cargo on board, while the Heather Bell, a steam lighter of 110 tons, was driven high and dry on the rocks with her back broken.

The plight of the *Alexandra* was a typical tale of those three days of fury. A refrigerating tender, she broke away from the eastern wharf to drift to the western side where she hugged the wall for several hours before being blown back towards the eastern side again, but not before running into the *S. S. Leura,* knocking a hole in its stern. She then drifted up harbour, ramming into the side of the *Star of Hope,* which promptly rolled over and sank, and herself ended up stranded on the rocks in front of the Pilot Station.

There were also tales of heroic seamanship. Captain R. Colbert of the *Bobbie Towns,* a steamer of 140 tons, displayed great skill in rescuing the *Diamantina,* a lighter of 285 tons, bringing her back to the eastern breakwater against all the fury of the cyclone, amid cheers from those on board the damaged *Leura.*

Many beche-de-mer cutters were sunk, total wrecks, but a few ships still at sea survived the blast. One of these was the schooner Scout under the command of Captain Campbell, which arrived in Townsville from Cairns on the 29th, after having anchored for three days between Goold and Hinchinbrook Islands. Another schooner, the *Lavina,* under Captain Paesch, was not so lucky. She left Townsville on Thursday evening of the 23rd, bound for Maryborough, but was forced to put back to anchor under Cape Cleveland. There she lost one anchor and, being unable to hold ground on the other, was driven before the gale to be totally wrecked on the shore of Magnetic Island on January 26th, 1896 — Magnetic's first real shipwreck. The spot where she came ashore was referred to as "Brights Bay" (near Hawkings Point), now known as Rocky Bay. One of her seamen, Frank Rawley, was struck by a wave and killed prior to the vessel striking the rocks. Survivors crawled over· the ridge to Harry Butler's place in Picnic Bay.

Another vessel to founder on Magnetic during cyclone "Sigma" was the *Lallah Rookh,* a ketch owned by Aplin, Brown and Crawshay Ltd. She arrived in Townsville Harbour from Cairns loaded with logs of timber, but drifted out of the breakwater area during the melee and was wrecked on Bremner Point near Arcadia. The "Sigma" cyclone caused a total of

£500,000 worth of damage to private homes, Harbour Board buildings, Council property, churches and other buildings in the town. Magnetic Island suffered severely, the surgery and a large store at the Quarantine Station at West Point being unroofed. Cape Cleveland lighthouse keeper's cottage was also unroofed.

Unlike the prolonged "Sigma", cyclone "Leonta" seven years later was very swift in its destructive action. The storm centre bore down on Townsville at a speed of 40 miles per hour and was all over in a day. The depression was originally reported a thousand miles off the coast north-east of Townsville, but moved so quickly it took everyone by surprise. A first-hand report of its progress was recorded by Charles S. Norris, Supreme Court Registrar in Townsville. He said that early in the morning of 9th March a moderate breeze from the south-west increased to a fresh breeze at 9 am, with ugly, threatening weather. At 9.15 am the barometer read 29.55 inches, and heavy rain squalls started in from the south-west. As some of these squalls crossed the Bay, they lifted spray to a considerable height, forming miniature water-spouts. By 11am the barometer had dropped to 29.30 and was still falling. The wind increased to hurricane force from the south-west at 1.30pm, when the barometer read 28.86, and it was noticed that the water in the Bay was blown out a long way from the shore, exposing bare sand for a distance much further than the lowest spring tides ever took it. A low pressure point of 28.61 was recorded at 2pm as the wind backed to the south-east and appeared to moderate slightly, only to scream in violently from the north in a short while, accompanied by heavy rain squalls. However, by 8pm the barometer was back up to 29.64 and the cyclone had passed on its devastating way.

Robert Hayles' jetty in Picnic Bay had been wrecked and huts unroofed, but damage in Townsville was even greater than that caused by "Sigma". The hospital, a substantial building, was largely demolished, most of its roofing having been torn off as well as solid brick walls collapsing on patients and burying them. Seven people were killed and hundreds injured. The Townsville Grammar School, another brick building, was completely destroyed; also the School of Arts building in Stanley St. Countless timber -frame private houses were smashed, together with churches, while the well known Queen's Hotel on the Strand was badly damaged. Shipping got off lightly compared with the "Sigma" rampage, apparently because of "Leonta's" shorter duration.

Thirty-seven years later, the Bulletin of Monday, February 19th, 1940, sadly lamented that Townsville's long immunity from cyclonic visitations had ended on the weekend. The centre of this one actually passed nearer to Ingham very early on Sunday morning of the 18th, when the barometer there fell to 28.50. An eye-witness account of 'The Elements' on this occasion, written by 'Cestus' , appeared in the paper:

> "Ever since the flame of the recent heat wave swept over us, the barometer has been steadily falling, unhurried, leisurely, but inexorably falling, and in that lay full threat. The horizon was leaden, grey, lethal as a crouching animal, ready to pounce and destroy: On Friday afternoon at 5.15 the glass read 29.55. At 6.30 on Saturday morning it had dropped to 29.45, at 1.30 it read 29.35 . ... Still falling at 5.00pm it read 29.20 and at 9.00pm 29.00. At 1.30 on Sunday morning the force of the wind was increasing and the glass showed 29.05. Rain was sheeting down and there was much weight in the wind which held southerly, with a tendency to west. Later it swung north-easterly.
>
> At daylight Sunday, visibility was confined to a few hundred yards ... The seas were short and upright, with no

> great send, but they had weight behind them. They swept the beaches mercilessly without pity ... The whole bay was a tumult of angry water, smashing across the breakwater in cascades of gleaming silver ... Castle Hill enshrouded in vapour, was weeping copiously at the toll of the storm. Down its pink grey granite side, water poured in gentle cascades."

Damage on Magnetic Island was more in the news this time. While the cyclone remained in the southern quarter, Picnic Bay was subjected to the full blast, and suffered heavily with tremendous scouring of the foreshore. The Picnic Bay Lifesaver's clubhouse, built at a cost of £850 and at its official opening in October 1938 said to be the most attractive building on the Island, was completely destroyed . At the peak of the cyclone, waves were breaking right over the building, undermining its entire foundations and causing its collapse. Hayles' second jetty at Picnic Bay was badly damaged that morning, most of its planking having been ripped off, though the piles still seemed to be secure. Nelly Bay jetty was almost completely wrecked, piles and all, including extensive washing out of the stone causeway approach along the rocky foreshore. It was sufficiently discouraging for Hayles' not to rebuild there again. Arcadia's relatively new jetty, on the other hand, suffered little damage-only a few planks missing, allowing passengers on an intrepid Hayles Sunday afternoon ferry (so soon after the cyclone!) to board the boat. The main difficulty for the skipper there was berthing in the huge swell. Considering that the peak of the cyclone passed over the Island during the early hours of the Sunday morning, the Bulletin of February 19th reported the incident quite matter-of-factly:

> "Hayles Magnetic service *Malita* made the voyage to Magnetic Island bays on Sunday afternoon under very adverse, but not dangerous conditions, and brought back

> to town a number of people who had dared the inclemency of the weather conditions during Saturday and made the trip to this popular resort. With the return of the boat in the evening came the first news of how the Island fared — passengers clambered over horizontal pieces from which decking was lost and reached the pier, but some less active passengers were brought out in a dinghy. A few passengers from Nelly Bay (where the jetty was completely wrecked) walked to Arcadia ..."

The protective wall at Alma Bay was brought down, along with the small bridge leading up to Alma Den guest-house. Arcadia Life-saver's clubhouse was badly damaged, along with other buildings. Small boat owners on the Island suffered heavy losses, one being the *Fox*, a 19 foot open boat with in-board motor owned by an Arcadian resident, which drifted out to sea as far as the 8th beacon in Platypus Channel before being driven back to Geoffrey Bay and smashed. Only the engine was salvaged.

Many houses were unroofed in Picnic Bay, although private dwellings in Arcadia and Nelly Bay suffered less damage, being well back from the beach in those bays where an effective wind-break was afforded by tree growth. A good deal of timber came down in most bays, including the telephone line poles to Horseshoe Bay. Horseshoe residents escaped with the lightest battering of all due to the predominantly southerly aspect of the cyclone's force, the Bay being shielded by the high hills of the centre of the Island.

Cyclones on the North Queensland coast are of course a yearly hazard — a continuing risk well known to its inhabitants. Yet it is an event of pure chance. Just where nature's most destructive wind force will hit the thousand mile Barrier Reef coastline is anyone's guess. Radar stations and weather satellites can track a cyclone's progress from its usual birth place, the Coral Sea. But once on course for a settled area there is nothing to be done but prepare oneself.

Friday, December 24th, 1971, became the most devastating Christmas Eve ever experienced on the Island. On the Thursday night, cyclone "Althea" was reported well out to sea. Heavy rain and wind gusts then were only a mild prelude to what was to follow after dawn. As daylight broke, fear commenced to grip the hearts of even the most experienced. By 9am buildings were suffering superficial damage, then half an hour later the wind reached a full pitch of fury. By 11am Magnetic Island and Townsville looked as if an atomic bomb had struck. Miraculously, "Althea" accounted for only three lives, but many more were injured and the community suffered unbelievable damage.

Ninety percent of the houses in Picnic Bay were wiped out, as were sixty percent in Nelly Bay and forty percent in Arcadia. Leaves were stripped from trees, water supplies severed and electricity cut, and people sought shelter in the few buildings left standing. In Townsville it was a similar story on a much grander scale, and shipping in Ross Creek became a mass of splintered and sunken derelicts. Most of the shipping damage was done by a Harbours Board dredge which broke its moorings at 10 am and ran amok among smaller craft. Insurance assessors estimated payouts of over ten million dollars.

Yet services were restored remarkably quickly. The Army came to the Islanders' assistance with special barge-loads of trucks carrying medical supplies, food and water, and reconstruction teams were deployed over the Island. Government assistance was immediate and generous, and the sadly tarnished image of a ruined resort was soon all but forgotten even by those who experienced it, as nature's strong healing pulse restored green leaves to the trees through the warmth, humidity and rainfall of an abnormally heavy wet season.

Picnic Bay Hotel Magnetic after Cyclone Althea

SHIPWRECKS

Magnetic Island has been described as a graveyard of forgotten ships. Many indeed are the still visible rotting remains of once proud hulls jutting out of the water around its various bays. But unromantic as it may be, very few of these wrecks actually occurred on the Island. Most were already useless hulks when towed to their final resting places to scar the beautiful beaches and bays. With all but a few exceptions they were brought in as intended breakwaters for small boat havens, only to eventually rust and crumble and become useless for that purpose, yet remain an eyesore for years.

Let us commence by listing the genuine shipwrecks which did actually founder on the Granite Isle. The earliest recorded was the already mentioned schooner *Lavina,* driven ashore in Rocky Bay at the height of cyclone "Sigma" in 1896, though other unrecorded smaller boats are likely to have come to grief on the Island before that. During the same storm, the ketch *Lallah Rookh* was wrecked on Bremner Point. Next was Robert Hayles' steam ferry the *Bee,* on Knobby Point in 1901 .

The *Norseman,* an iron lighter of 80 tons, owned by Burns Philp, came near to being wrecked in Horseshoe Bay in a gale on 5th February, 1893. She was carrying sand ballast to sailing vessels there, and was blown out of anchorage to be finally wrecked in Cleveland Bay. Robert Hayles' third boat, the Magnet, which was eventually sold to Alf Leone, was wrecked in Florence Bay on a date unknown, parts of the wreckage still lying there under water. But apart from small boats wrecked in the 1940 cyclone, that appears to be all Magnetic can claim as her own spoils.

The *"Presto",* another casualty of the "Sigma" cyclone, wrecked in Townsville Harbour, was purchased soon after by William Bright of Nelly Bay, who had it dumped off Bright Point for a shelter from the sou'easter at his landing . She is still visible at low tide today — dangerous looking, rusted iron ribs jutting out of the sand just below the water surface — a hazard to the unwary navigator.

A similar fate befell the *George Rennie* at Picnic Bay. Originally used by Howard Smith Ltd as a lighter to freight cargo from the North Anchorage hear Magnetic Island to the Port in the early days before the breakwater and harbour, she was bought by a Mr Garner and beached at Picnic Bay in the lee of Hawkins Point for 'shelter' purposes.

The hulk Presto, dumped in Nelly Bay as a breakwater in the early 1920's

Yet another 'shelter' was the *Moltke,* a German barque used in overseas trade, now a navigational hazard near Arcadia wharf. She struck a reef off Cape Bowling Green while southward bound after discharging cargo at Townsville. In spite of being badly holed, the ship was patched up and re-floated, to be towed back to Townsville where the Burns Philp Company used her as a coal hulk stationed at the old North Anchorage. In 1913 Dr McCabe, the dentist of Arcadia, bought her as a protection for his own Geoffrey Bay landing. The story goes that *Moltke* was towed into position by the Tug *Resolute* and got ready to be blown up by charges at the water-line. It seems that the demolition expert had consumed a few too many drinks with Dr McCabe on board the Tug on the way over, for he lit the fuses on *Moltke* prematurely — while the Tug still had her in tow, and before she had been anchored in position. The Tug skipper, alarmed at the shout of 'fire' from the explosives man who was already rowing away, hastily cast off the hulk in order to get his Tug-boat clear of danger. Meanwhile, the vagaries of the tide drifted Moltke further out into the channel before she sank — a position in which her value as shelter was negligble and her danger to small craft considerable. She is still there, now marked by two piles.

It is presumed that both the *Palmosa* in Horseshoe Bay, and the *Platypus* in Arthur Bay (the old dredge), were also intended as 'shelters', although no details are available. The *Octopus,* an ex Harbour Board bucket-dredge built in 1882, was beached temporarily for some years at Nelly Bay-between 1922 and 1928. An early photograph of the old walk-way of Nelly Bay jetty shows the ship hulk in the background, not far from the present bathing enclosure. Jack Murray, a boat builder there, wanted to salvage all her copper and good timber. In 1928 Hayles Magnetic towed her away again after her bottom had been cemented in to refloat her, and she was sunk in a deep rocky cove off the eastern side of the Island. Another ship to be stripped earlier by Jack Murray was the barque *Tyburnia* in 1901. Much sound timber-beautiful 10" X 6" teak planks — were obtained from her before she was finally beached at Townsville in front of Queen's Hotel for purposes unknown.

Most obvious of all Magnetic Island's wrecks for many years was the *City of Adelaide,* sitting gauntly upright in the mud at Cockle Bay. Being a large vessel (1, 112 tons) she was a real landmark against the mangroves, but is now well rusted and rapidly disintegrating. Originally a brig-rigged steamer brought out from Scotland in 1864, she was used by the Australian Steam Navigation Company in passenger service between Melbourne and Sydney, and later to Honolulu and San Francisco, until 1885.

Arcadia jetty about 1920, with the hulk Moltke sunk there as a breakwater

She remained idle for four years until 1889, a period during which her owners suffered financial set-backs. A Mr Ritchie bought her in 1889 and converted her to a four-masted sailing barque, by removing her engines and boilers. *City of Adelaide* then went back into the coastal trade for a few years, but was eventually sold to Howard Smith Company in Townsville, who used her as a coal hulk for ten years. In 1912 her coal cargo ignited and burnt for several days before being put out, after which she was replaced.

George Butler (Harry's son) bought the stripped hull of *City of Adelaide* in 1916, again with the idea of using the big hulk as a breakwater for his Picnic Bay jetty. While being towed across the Bay she encountered heavy weather and went aground inadvertently at Cockle Bay. George then apparently got the notion to fit her up as a novel weekend resort just where she was, but the First World War was still under way and the scheme was dropped. Later generations have used her as a swimming pool, fishing platform and navigational marker when sailing down the West Channel. At the time she was first brought to Townsville it was sa id that her original log -books, covering her entire history, were still in one of the cabins. However, these maritime records meant nothing to the strippers, who burned them as fuel in the old ferry plying across Ross Creek in Townsville.

The hulk City of Adelaide resting on the mud at Cockle Bay since 1916, photographed in 1970. Rust at the high tide mark has almost eaten through the hull

CHAPTER 6
PINEAPPLES

Magnetic Island was at one time renowned for the quality of its pineapples. The pineapple plant likes a warm, but not too wet climate, and Magnetic Island fits the bill admirably. Frosts during the winter months in some of the now bigger pineapple growing areas of southern Queensland, set back their plants, and their rainfall is at times excessive. If the fruit has too much moisture supplied the full flavour is not developed. A point also in favour of the Island fruit is the absence of any artificial ripening processes.

In the early days before artificial hormone ripening was practised in the south, northern fruit was always first to ripen naturally, and came in on the southern markets at a time when it would command a good price. Nowadays the big canneries are more than amply supplied by southern growers whose freight problems are minimal, and during the 1950's the

Magnetic Island industry slumped considerably. Rising freight cost was the prime reason for the demise of the majority of Island growers who, apart from mainland rail costs, had to bear local ferry charges. However, one needs only to sample a Magnetic 'pine' grown in somebody's private allotment, to testify to their excellent flavour.

Pineapple growing in Australia started about 1838 with a few plants brought from India to a German mission station near Brisbane. The centre of early commercial growing was on the steep hillsides of Woombye and Nambour, 75 miles north of Brisbane, near the Sunshine Coast. Of interest is the fact that the now large pineapple industry in the Hawaiian Islands was mainly initiated with plants brought from Queensland in 1896.

The pineapple is an extremely hardy form of growth, being akin to the cactus family in its ability to survive for lengthy periods without water. The plant will actually remain alive for many months without contact with the soil, for the fleshy-natured leaves have large water-storage cells in their make-up, enabling the plant to withstand drought. There are no doubt many southerners who, never having seen the Queen of tropical fruit salad constituents growing, will have no idea of the plant itself. There have been people who imagined that the fruit grew under the soil like a carrot, with only the top bunch of leaves showing above ground. As the planting of tops is one of the methods used for regeneration, this is perhaps understandable. Actually, the fruit is borne on a single stalk growing up from the base of a concentric formation of long, pointed leaves, which extend to a height of about three feet from the ground.

Jessie Macqueen had an amusing anecdote to relate concerning an old scally-wag who made the most of such ignorance during the heyday of Magnetic Island's pineapple fame. One day a party of tourists came to his old hut in the bush, which was surrounded by several big stands of wild Pandanus palms (a prickly-leafed tree with 'walking leg' type exposed roots, very common in the bush on Magnetic). Each tree was heavy with huge, redd ish -tinged, golden -yellow fruit, two or three times the size and weight of a normal pineapple, but almost identical in shape and appearance. The visitors asked the old fellow incredulously if these were pineapples. Barely able to keep a straight face, he assured them that they were — the best crop he'd had for some time in fact. Yes, they could have one for five shillings apiece if they liked, he said, picking one of the monstrous fruit for closer examination. Impressed, and taken in by earlier stories of the gigantic size of the Island fruit, the whole party bought one each. They staggered back down to the beach with their heavy booty, while the old man chuckled at the thought of those hard useless nuts.

There may have been some small consolation for the victims had they known of the Aborigines' recipe for treating the big fibrous nuts to make them edible, though it is doubtful if the result would have been as appetizing as the juicy fruit they desired.

There are three main groups of the cultivated pineapple family — the Cayenne, the Queen and the Spanish. The smooth-leafed Cayenne variety is the most widely grown in Australia, for canning purposes particularly, although it is also a deliciously juicy table fruit. The Ripley Queen, or rough-leafed variety, is grown more especially for the fresh fruit market, as it has a higher sugar content and a rich yellow flesh. Being smaller than the Cayenne, the fruit is not quite so suitable for canning. The Red Spanish pineapple, the main variety grown in Cuba and Puerto Rico, is not represented in Australia.

On Magnetic Island the Cayenne and Queen are distinguished merely by the names "smooth" and "rough" respectively, this feature referring to the nature of the leaves of the parent plant. The "rough" has many more spines along the whole length of its slightly reddish-coloured leaves, whereas the darker-green leaves of the "smooth" have only a few spines near the tip, the rest of the leaf being smooth-edged. The larger, extremely juicy "smooths" have a palate-tingling tartness compared to the sweeter, more solid flesh of the "rough".

The dense, shallow root system of the pineapple is concentrated mainly in the top six inches of soil, which must be well-drained, preferably on a slope and in an area where no frosts are likely, as it is most definitely a sun-lover. The sandy loam of Magnetic Island's soil is eminently suited to the plant's requirements. There are four methods of propagation possible, all requiring the planting by hand of material from the origin al plant. The most well known method is to use tops from ripe fruit planted a couple of inches into the soil, though this method takes longer to produce a crop. The usual plantation method is to use either suckers or slips. A sucker is a purely vegetative side-shoot arising from the main stem. If closely examined, juvenile roots may be seen already forming in the close-packed lay of the bottom leaves of the sucker after it is broken off from the parent plant. Suckers can be all sizes, the larger ones being sometimes almost as big as the plant it was taken from. The normal time taken for a plant to mature and bear fruit under this method is eighteen months, although in the northern tropics as on the Island, where both summer and winter temperatures are higher, thus al lowing a longer growing period each year, a good sucker can produce fruit within twelve months.

Slips, or gill-sprouts, are a third alternative planting material. These are small, curled sprouts of leaf-like bunches, growing out of the base of the fruit stalk, sometimes referred to as "robbers" because too many of them rob the fruit of sustenance. Slip planting is most advantageous where planting material has to be transported long distances, as they are the smallest offshoot available from the parent plant. Occasion ally a fourth method is used — that of planting butts or stems of mature plants which have already borne fruit, but this method can produce a very uneven crop.

The double-row system of planting is the usual method in Queensland, where two rows of plants are spaced two feet apart, with twelve inches between individual plants in the rows. The double rows are then spaced six feet apart centre to centre, giving about 14,000 plants to the acre. The reason for double rows is to avoid excessive weed growth, and to conserve soil moisture with the greater area of leaf cover thus afforded. In the early days of pineapple cultivation it was common to keep a plant producing for up to eight years or more, but recent commercial practice is to retain a plantation for only two successive crops, as later fruit tends to become smaller and less prolific. This means in effect that one can expect the first crop of fruit after 18 months, and the first ratoon in a further 12 to 18 months, giving a full cycle of planting every 3 to 3½ years.

Many years ago it was accidentally discovered that ordinary fire-smoke drifting across a pineapple plantation would bring plants into flower prematurely. Researchers then tried acetylene-gas as a stimulant for early production of fruit, and this method using calcium carbide generators was practised commercially for some time.

Nowadays, planters find it more convenient to use a chemical hormone preparation known a& ANA (Alpha Naphthalene Acetic acid) to induce fruiting at times most convenient to markets, but not necessarily convenient to the plant itself, or to the final flavour of the fruit.

Pineapples at Horseshoe Bay

The pineapple flower is a wonderfully complex group of tiny blue petals in each small eye of the dark-green coloured budding fruit. A complete mini-version of the mature fruit in fact, gaily adorned with the blue flowers over its surface, and crowned with a midget tuft of green leaves. The centre leaves of the parent plant show a distinct reddish tinge surrounding the little 'pin e-let' at this stage. Gradually the flowers disappear as the fruit fattens into a large barrel shape on the end of its stem, the top tuft of leaves growing with the rest, until it finally shows light yellow patches at maturity. There would hardly be a home-gardener on Magnetic Island these days who does not have his own plot of 'pines', and the first fruit he picks is bound to be the most delicious he has ever tasted.

A man who came to farm pineapples on Magnetic just a little too late to cash in on the biggest bonanza was Arthur

Rollason of Horseshoe Bay. Nevertheless, Arthur and his family made a comfortable living at the game during the early post-war years — enough to build a pleasant home near the main road into Horseshoe Bay. He first took a look at the island during the depression years, when many of the old-timers were still at Horseshoe — George Apjohn, George Dench and Bill Swenson among them. He recalled that George Apjohn, the giant whose feats we have already mentioned, owned an 18 foot boat at one time, in which he would occasionally go across to Townsville. A couple of hours prior to sailing, George would blow an almighty blast on a bugle, echoing around the Bay, to warn those who wanted to accompany him to be ready.

At the peak of the pineapple boom during the 1930's, Arthur said there would sometimes be up to 3,000 cases of 'pines' at a time, stacked on Arcadia wharf ready for shipment. A magazine article of that period reported an estimated 33,000 cases of fruit shipped out each year from the Island . It was not only pineapples either. Many other fruits were successfully grown in the rich, loamy soil which was so common in newly opened up land then: all kinds of citrus of excellent quality, mangoes, paw-paws, granadillas, bananas, passion fruit and so on. The growers did not even have to plough the land in the beginning. After clearing and burning of stumps, planting material would be just hand-mattocked into the chocolate loam. There was such a demand for planting material that anything they could lay their hands on would be used — suckers, gills or tops. Some suckers fruited after only 8 months, while the gills would have grown to such a tremendous size by the time they matured at 18 months, that Arthur recalls having trouble on occasions trying to stuff two huge pineapples into a sugar bag.

While Arthur was working on Bill Swenson's farm (near the guesthouse) in the early years, he operated a unique home-made juice extractor, constructed of lengths of 3" by 2" hardwood bolted together to allow them to rotate past each other. Pineapples would be sliced into three or four big chunks and crushed in this crude machine, juice pouring out through drilled holes in the timber to be caught and sold to appreciative tourists for sixpence a glass.

The land and soil was not looked after as it should have been, however. Repeated burning and heavy, leaching , wet-season rains carried away tons of top-soil, until production on some farms fell right off. During the war years when fruit was in high demand, growers got away with almost anything. In a dry year when pines may have been hardly bigger than apples, with stunted little tops, they were still getting £6 a case. Many men rounded off their fortunes at this time, then, having plundered the land without putting anything back into it, sold out and left. The industry finally collapsed, and only the true connoisseur — the taster of a superior juice — would lament.

The slopes of Mt. Cook (double hump on far left) are densely forested, with patches of rain forest jungle occurring in some of the moister valleys on the eastern side of the range. Arua Peak on right.

CHAPTER 7
MOUNT COOK

Mount Cook, the highest point on the skyline of Magnetic Island at 496 metres (1,628 feet), perpetuates the name of the Island's famous discoverer, though it is doubtful whether Cook himself was very impressed with the great mass of forest-covered land which forms a fairly indistinct summit on the central high plateau of the Isle. He did not bother to name it anyway, for that was left to the early surveyors.

Some idea of the geography of the mountain may be got by a description of a climb up what has been called the 'goat-track' route immediately above upper Gustav Creek. Leaving the big white paperbark trees of Gustav Creek behind, one climbs steeply along a ridge leading up from the south-eastern side of the mountain. The vegetation change on the way up is quite remarkable for a mountain of such modest height. Poplar gums, white gums, bloodwoods, wattles and pandanus of the valley floor soon give way to scrubbier growths, including a defined patch of kapok trees. The latter bear large bright yellow flowers on almost bare, rounded limbs, devoid of leaves in the Dry Season. Later in the season when the sparse foliage reappears, the flowers lose their petals to become shiny green pods which gradually turn brown, then swell and burst open to reveal the silken kapok fibres in side.

White-cedar trees stand out amongst the other growth on the foothills, with their lighter green foliage and mottled, scale-like bark. Although they do not eat the leaves of this tree, koalas are often observed resting in convenient limbs of the cedar. Two colonies of koalas lived close to our home in Gustav Valley, calling their guttural grunting noises of an evening. The cry of the male could be described as the grunt of a stuttering pig! At a time of mating of a moonlit evening, the deep-toned stutters echoed back and forth across the valley between colonies. The koala was introduced to Magnetic by Bob Hayles in the 1920's.

The possums which have increased to almost pest proportions on the Island were probably also introduced by man, although some say they entered naturally, drifting across from the mainland on flood debris. The pretty little black-tailed rock-wallaby will often be disturbed in the bush during the day, and if one is fortunate an echidna (spiny ant-eater) may also be seen. At least one should be able to see their scooped-out burrows in the earth along the trail.

Resuming our mountain climb and progressing further up the ridge, we note here and there the tell-tale piles of a black-skinned fruit lying on the ground — the Burdekin plum. The fruit is about the same size as an ordinary plum, but thinner fleshed over a large, hard stone. Birds delight in the flesh which tastes not unlike the Quandong or wild peach, common in the Mallee country of South Australia. Many people ripen the fruit in paper bags and eat them either raw or stewed. Burdekin plum timber has a beautiful grain and has been used for furniture.

All kinds of creeping vines inhabit the jungle at the most inconvenient spots for a bushwalker-tentacle-like 'wait-awhiles' (lawyer-vine), prickly-thorned stems of variety past description lie in wait for the unwary. Above about 200 metres altitude one must watch out for the stinging-plant *Laportea Moroides*. This spindly looking shrub with large, heart-shaped, succulent, light-green leaves with serrated edge, can inflict a very painful sting, as more than one unfortunate has discovered! W. D. Francis describes the culprit in his book "Australian Rain Forest Trees" thus:

> "*Laportea Moroides* — stinging shrub. Does not attain tree size. Leaves similar in shape to those of *Laportea Gigas* (giant Gympie Stinging Tree found in southern Queensland) but can be distinguished from them by being mostly peltate ... The sting of this shrub is the most severe of the East Australian nettles."

The heart-shaped leaf of *Laportea* is covered with myriads of fine hairs, each one a minute poison tube which breaks off in the skin upon being brushed. Apart from the severe pain at the time, the sting is long-lasting, the affected area remaining sensitive for up to a fortnight afterwards. One is constantly reminded of it when under the shower, the original pain being re -induced by the water. One learns by hard experience though, and to the observant there are warning signs in the presence of similar looking shrubs growing in the same locality as *Laportea* in the moist gullies on the south-eastern side of the mountain.

Approaching a level of about 300 metres the vegetation change is marked, with many ferns and palms appearing. The bracken fern is common, with other ferns and lilies and tree-orchids in the darker, overhanging rainforest type jungle. In these shady gullies the Fan palm and Cabbage palm *Livistona Australis* flourish, the latter looking very much like a coconut palm as Captain Cook mentioned on the Palm Islands.

Close-up, though, they are seen to have a smooth green trunk for a few feet at the top near the base of the leaf stems, while the fruit is a small brown seed carried on lacy fronds like a date palm.

The stinging plant, Laportea Moroides

The Umbrella tree is common, jutting out of crevices in huge granite rocks on the ridge. Some of these rocks are almost totally entwined with wild-fig tree roots, clinging and conforming to the surface like huge serpents constricting their prey. They make good hand-holds while climbing among the rock caverns, as do the long vine ropes dangling free from the tree tops, inviting a Tarzan-style trapeze act. Bamboos of a long, slender variety entangle themselves amongst this intricate web of suspended stems, making for a continuing tussle in forcing a way through.

The old misshapen Hoop pine trees *Araucaria Cunninghamii,* which appear all over the Island (often mistaken by visitors for the Norfolk Island pine, which has a more regular form), grow mainly on the ridge tops away from the denser jungle of the gullies, standing in proud relief on the skyline above all the lesser timber. In spite of the Hoop pine's liking for exposed positions, it does seem to have an upper limit in altitude, for none are seen on the topmost plateau around 400 metres.

The undulating central high mass of the Island is dominated by Forest-sheoak trees (as distinct from the species of sheoak seen along the foreshore), which cover the area to the almost complete exclusion of other trees in many places. Their fine, pine-like needles litter the floor of the forest, preventing much undergrowth and allowing easier walking under the shady canopy. A few Black-boy or Yacka plants grow in sunny positions among the rocks on the high spots.

Summit of Arua Peak, Nelly Bay below

The 'goat-track' has now taken us to the top of Arua Peak (350 m), which is a great ledge of bare rock standing clear of tree growth and affording an almost 360 degree view of the surrounds — one of the best vantage points on the Island, better than Mt Cook itself. The whole of the eastern half of Magnetic Island is within compass from this peak, enabling one to appreciate with some reality one's position on an island in the ocean.

About twenty kilometres to the east can be seen the white tower of Cape Cleveland lighthouse standing at the tip of a long, narrow jutting peninsula of hills, and beyond that, the broad expanse of Bowling Green Bay in the far distance. Almost due south on the mainland skyline is the television mast on Mt Stuart at 600 metres, while directly below it on the plains surrounding the bare rocks of Castle Hill, sprawls the city of Townsville and its port, with the long breakwater arms reaching out towards Platypus Channel.

The tree-covered summit of our goal, Mount Cook, rises two peaks further west of Arua Peak; another half-hour's scramble down into a small saddle and along the topmost ridge of the Island to the summit rock-cairn hidden away in the bush. Under this small cairn two aluminium canisters contain the names of all past conquerors.

Harry Butler was probably the first white man to climb the mountain, and Jessie Macqueen describes her own climb to Mount Cook with Nell Butler and two other girls in the early 1900's. They chose a rough, long route indeed -from the Butler home at Picnic Bay straight across the rugged granite ridges to the summit, involving a tortuous up and down struggle over many hills between. Of course at this time there was no track into Gustav Creek at Nelly Bay, which would have enabled them to get closer in to the mountain's lower slopes.

Although they set out before day-break with a picnic hamper, the girls were not to return until midnight. Harry Butler warned them that dresses would be no good for such a venture in rough bush, so they each purchased a pair of men's dungaree trousers and thick shoes for the occasion. Jessie recalled passing a clear running stream just after lunch, where they dangled tired feet in little rock-pools, only to have their toes nibbled at by fresh-water lobsters.

As the long, exhausting afternoon wore on, Gwenneth began to doubt whether she'd make it, and queried Nell, their guide, "When, for goodness' sake, do we stop climbing the wrong mountains?" But Nell knew where she was going and pointed to the summit above. They were nearly there, and Jessie Macqueen records:

> "Just below Mt Cook we halted under a grove of Sheoaks on a miniature plateau of about half an acre thickly carpeted with dried pine needles and cones the discard of many years. An unexpected and pleasant sight these well grown oaks. Keeping to themselves so to speak and not ming ling with commonfolk trees growing around their select holding. Soon then we really ascended to reach our goal and stand on the topmost peak of Mt Cook after a memorable exciting climb not previously attempted by females and not by many of the opposite sex outside the Butler family and official surveyors of the early seventies."

Having arrived very late in the day, Nell urged the party to hurry on the descent lest darkness should overtake them. But despite short cuts through gorges instead of over ridges, and sliding on their trouser bottoms down steep inclines, they were only a third of the way home by nightfall. Wary of the party becoming separated in the dark, Nell kept them close together as she guided them on their stumbling way.

Maudie soon complained that she could go no further because the soles of her shoes were flapping and tripping her up. "Well, if you don't walk," said Nell dryly, "you'll just have to sleep on the mountain." Maudie, terrified at the thought, pleaded to hold Nell's hand for the rest of the way.

While still well up on the ridges they saw the lights of Picnic Bay and started to coo-ee. When faint coo-ees were heard in reply, the girls sang songs loudly, as much to boost their own morale as to guide the menfolk who set out up the mountainside with lanterns to search for them. It was midnight when four exhausted climbers with wildly dishevelled hair, clothes torn to shreds, limbs bruised and scratched, yet nevertheless triumphant, were met by Grandad and the others. They sat down to an overdue dinner and ate ravenously before Grandad sitting at the head of the table with, as Jessie Macqueen says:

> "... his flowing white beard spread across the brown arms where they rested upon the table. He said little at first but the fine old eyes seemed to hold a whimsical expression until I referred to the group of sheoaks we encountered atop the mountain. His head shot up at that and his eyes opened in genuine surprise. 'Oh!' he said slowly as he always spoke, 'so you got to those sheoaks did you?' 'Yes,' I said. 'Do you know them Grandad?' 'Yes, I know them well,' he said, 'and if you girls got as far as those oaks, well then you really did get to the top of Mt Cook. We didn't think you'd make it and when it got late we thought one of you had an accident and the others standing by. Humph! so you found the sheoaks did you?' Now his eyes held admiration for the three of us but were filled with an expression of deep pride as they rested upon Nell. Inspired perhaps by the generous reception of a

masculine audience our inner feelings might be described as Virtuous Elation."

Another early climber to Mount Cook was Martin Carlson of Fish Cove, who first ascended it in 1924 with a few friends. At that time he discovered a permanent spring not far below the summit of what he called 'Pyramid Peak' (Arua Peak), in a beautiful gorge of green palms and ferns now referred to as Palm Gorge. This unique spring of crystal clear water, nearly 300 metres up the mountainside in upper Gustav Valley, continues to flow through the driest months on the Island, long after many wells in settled areas have gone dry.

Death Adders will occasionally be seen on the mountain - mostly sluggish and slow to awaken from their curled up spot on the trail. The flattened, rather short body has a worm-like rear end, and a blunt lizard-like head. It comes fourth on the list of Australia's death-dealing snakes — Taipan, Tiger and King Brown rating more dangerous. None of the latter are found on the Island. Much more common are the spotted rock-pythons (non-poisonous), and various species of harmless treesnakes, bright yellow-bellied, green bodies coiled around trees in some home gardens.

A walk right across the Island beyond Mount Cook will take one into a steep, rough area where the vegetation eventually thins out amongst big rock outcrops on the northern slopes of the Isle. This northern side is much drier looking than the eastern and southern slopes of the mountain, presumably because most rain is precipitated on the south-eastern side from the prevailing east and south-east winds. Great clumps of spinifex grass inject their sharp-pointed needles into bare legs, as one has· no choice but to sink down into a mass of it in order to traverse a steep rock face. One emerges on the Five Beach

Bay coastline, a series of unspoiled little sand coves which eventually lead right around to Horseshoe Bay.

An easier and more well known walk is the graded track from Upper Mandalay Avenue in Nelly Bay, around to Arcadia via the Horseshoe Bay Lookout and Sphinx Lookout. It offers many pleasant open views of the Island as well as the chance of seeing some of the birds and animals in the wild. Other well marked walks are to Balding Bay from the eastern end of Horseshoe Bay and to Maud Bay from the western end of Horseshoe Bay.

NATIONAL PARK

That area of Magnetic Island considered as unsuitable for normal avenues of development (fortunately the major part) was declared a National Park in 1953. This criterion has probably been the deciding factor for most parks world wide — the land which man cannot bend to his will easily-but even then he may already have plundered the best of its tall timber. Thereafter, complete protection of all native flora and fauna is enforced within the region. But there remains the most serious threat of all-fire. This is also the most difficult to guard against, because man himself is usually the culprit.

Repeated bush-fires over the years have permanently destroyed some small unique pockets of rain-forest growth in certain valleys on the Island, rain-forest being particularly susceptible to fire. The more open and hardy eucalypt forests usually regenerate after a burn, but tender young sapling regrowth is eventually killed altogether and even the parent trees finally succumb. Many rain -forest constituents are killed by even the slightest exposure to an adjacent high temperature forest fire. Early photographs of the Island indicate that the natural cover of vegetation has been denuded quite extensively, especially near settlements. The Horseshoe Bay area in particular has been subjected to much burning off of arable land, with consequent accidental spread of bush-fires into the hills. 'It's OK,' they say, 'it always burns itself out once it reaches the hills!'

Large tracts of hillside become barren areas, exposing large granite boulders formerly covered by tall trees and held there by a stable root system. The tree becomes ash and the loose, stony soil , open now to the full glare of tropical sun, is easily scoured by the erosive effect of heavy wet season rains . Down tumbles the boulder, and with it all the humus and firm body in the top cover of soil. A patch on the hillside where once a tall forest giant was cremated — a broad line of white ash marks the grave — is a spot now rendered infertile by the intense heat of a glowing log. That spot will not grow anything for years. The crumbling effects of water erosion causes more undermining of rocks and boulders, so that a climber must be wary indeed as to which stone he entrusts his weight.

There is a certain apathy and resignation toward what many people on the Island regard as an entirely inevitable annual event in the dry season. But how do these fires start? There are many causes, such as cigarette butts, etc., which are preventable. However, it is depressing to see just how often so-called 'controlled burns' get out of control. The owner of a block, being too lazy to cut the long, dry grass on his acres, decides to strike a match in stead. A sudden gust of unexpected wind carries a flare of burning gas over into the bush, and the holocaust is launched.

It is said by some that it sweeps the bush clean — a tonic to the soil, replacing certain elements. But by far the greater quantity of original grass material disappears skywards as gases in a burn, and is lost. Such pitifully small amounts of barren ash to which the potentially fertile humus and decaying vegetation are reduced, can do little to replenish the natural growth before heavy rains carry it and the surrounding soil right away, to be swept into the streams and eventually out to sea. The greatest proportion of nutriment for plant life is derived from the atmosphere itself, assisted by water and humus action in the roots, the mineral requirements being minute and present in the decaying straw anyway if left unburned. Many North Queensland graziers are now becoming aware of the beneficial effects of not burning grazing land — retention of moisture in the soil under decaying vegetation to stimulate quality grass growth. Some fire advocates will point to the welcome green shoots springing up everywhere among the ugly, blackened stalks after a burn. But these green shoots are merely the latest regrowth of the same tough, rank, useless species of spear-grass and the like, being the only survivors of the searing inferno. The fine, soft-stemmed natural grasses, food for the wallabies (or the grazier's sheep and cattle) are completely destroyed, seeds and all, in the top layer of soil, so allowing the rank species to grow even thicker and higher for the following season, to become an even greater fire hazard. These coarse, hollow-stem, tall straws make highly inflammable fuel, unlike the finer, wispy-stemmed native constituents just above ground level.

The Aborigines may have used fire occasionally for hunting, but it is clear that unlike the white man who has an obsession for burning-off every year regardless, resulting often in bush fires which come close to destroying the whole Island, the Aborigines were more careful with nature's living forest and everything it contained. If the Australian Aboriginal was as reckless with fire as the proponents of burning would have us believe, it is certain that in over 40,000 years of occupation, places like Magnetic Island would long ago have been reduced to bare rock. Yet, early pioneers like Harry Butler described it as heavily forested from mountain top to beachside. In a mere 100 years the white man has brought the vegetation to the verge of complete barrenness, to the point where the only hope of regeneration of the old forest, the delicate tree seed lings, are being repeatedly destroyed. It could reach the stage soon, when the adult trees finally succumb, that there may not even be any seeds left.

The fuel reduction burning practised by Forestry officials all over Australia, is detrimental to the long term future of natural forests. In the end, it creates and sustains, a fire-hungry environment, as the fire-tender species are eliminated. It is well known that many smaller birds disappear altogether from such an environment, as a result of destruction of the understorey shrubs in which they shelter and nest.

As a solution to Magnetic Island's problem, it would not impose a great burden on anyone to outlaw burning-off operations altogether, including so-called 'controlled' official burn-offs which get away as often as the others. A minimum amount of grass cutting can ensure complete fire protection of buildings and property, especially on this Island where growth during the dry winter months is negligible. Once cut, it will remain clear for long periods. Getting the fire-warden's permission to burn off an area is hardly a fool-proof way of preventing bush-fires. No need to risk burning a whole island because someone is too lazy to cut a firebreak.

CHAPTER 8
BIRDS

On Magnetic Island the sound of birds replaces the roar of the city — a visitor who has any interest in wildlife could not fail to notice it. The bird variety must be described as prodigious on this mountainous, forested Isle, unlike on some of the flat out-reef coral cay resorts and smaller Islands where the species are limited. A total of 189 different species have been sighted.

The most characteristic sounds in the bush-covered valleys and around settlement fringes, and even in the centres of housing areas, are the eerily distinctive wail of the Bush curlew at night and the loud notes of the Pied currawong during the day. The currawong often calls while in flight, making the sound carry through the trees-a ringing, "Clung-a -clung-clung, clung-a-clung-clung." or a single, "Coo-wah-ah," as the big black-plumaged bird (with traces of white on wing tips and tail) wings his way to a nearby house to collect any meat or fruit scraps offering. Generally in company with the currawong is the Helmeted frair-bird or Leatherhead, with its long skinny neck and black friar-capped head making a harsher, "Cwu-aak," call.

The Bush stone curlew, also known as the Thick-knee, could almost be regarded as Magnetic Island's own symbol. The bird is now rare in many southern parts of Australia, yet there would be no corner of the Island where its unmistakable wail, sounding like some long lost spirit of the dark, could not be heard of an evening. This is due, no doubt, to the complete absence of mainland predators such as the fox and dingo. The bird should not be confused with the closely related Beach stone curlew, or the Eastern curlew which, like the curved-bill Whimbrel family, inhabit the sea-shores. All of the latter are also found on the Island. The bush curlew's habitat is open forest country. The Aborigines called it the 'Weeloo', and its weird, heart-rending wail has also given rise to the name 'Screaming-woman bird'. For those who wish to be in no doubt as to its id entity, the scientific name is Burhinus Magnirostris. With a body about sixteen inches long, of grey-brown speckled plumage, large eyes, and straight, long bill, it stands on long skinny legs which have prominent knee joints and three widely spaced toes. It is a ground-dwelling bird, but will when disturbed, flutter off for a short distance before returning to the ground as soon as possible.

The curlew is not difficult to befriend and many people on the Island have a favourite bird come in from the bush regularly to feed as a 'pet'. One such attached itself to our household in the upper Gustav Valley. 'Susie', as she was christened, was given to us as a youngster after her mother was run over by a car, having been dazzled in the headlights one evening. Such accidents can happen only too easily, unfortunately, as the birds stand and stare at an approaching vehicle. Susie identified completely with humans — not unreasonable for a ground-dweller. She was fed meat scraps, cheese, insects hand-caught around a lamp at night, as well as hordes of the sluggish March flies in season, which are not difficult to slap dead around one's legs in the daytime. Susie would rush in for the kill at sound of the slap. She became to us as a pet dog, following us around everywhere and running to greet us when we came home from an outing.

With head held erect and beak opened wide, the weeloo emits a piercing, smooth-volumed scream in reply to another's distant challenge. The wail is climaxed with rapid beating of wings and fanned out tail as the sound changes to an excited pulsating chorus in unison with other birds. Occasionally the call is a shorter, half-hearted plaintive "Mee-oww" like a kitten. Observing a group of these birds during a typical 'corroboree', one wonders whether ·their act may not have inspired our aborigines as much as the well known Brolga's dance. A performing bird will sometimes stand encircled by a bevy of barrackers who eventually join it in the dance.

There is more to the story of our pet curlew Susie. She never allowed strangers to actually touch or pat her — an annoying human habit, she considered. Yet she would voluntarily walk right up to a person's bare feet and nibble at toes without hesitation. Daylight hours were spent under the house or in the shade of a tree in a half-sitting position with eyes closed, dozing. Every evening she came to the back door for her share of our meal, and if we were forgetful, started up a 'tweeting' reminder. Though she consumed fair quantities her figure did not suffer, and she retained her natural slim wild form.

When we first adopted the waif . her sole vocabulary was a series of excited squawks and flapping of wings at feeding time. Then one evening after she began to mature, a wild curlew uttered its wail close by. Susie straightened up immediately, head held high, big eyes blinking, as some instinctive recognition flitted through her brain. Perhaps she wasn't human after all, the eyes seemed to say. She tried to reply with a comical, squeaky wail. Gradually over the next few days she perfected it — head held erect, beak wide open, she emitted the earsplitting scream right under our noses, even to the excited beating of wings and fanned out tail.

'Susie' the author's pet Bush Curlew at upper Gustav Creek

Susie learned to fly the long, shallow gliding flight of her kind and often went walkabout as she got older, but always returned to bow to the ground in front of us, chirping away with her 'talking' call. She was quite fearless of the motor-mower when I cut the grass, for she would follow me around the lawn, diving head first at a disturbed insect the very second the mower wheels rolled past full blast within an inch of her frail body.

It took a fair bit to upset Susie, but whenever she did become alarmed, her head feathers would erect as her neck bent low to a horizontal posit ion, while she uttered a low purring sound. Such was her reaction to being hounded by our stupid turkeys. Turkeys, being intensely curious birds, will walk up in a mob to anything strange, heads cocked to one side, investigating. Of course they soon got to know Susie, but for some reason .would not tolerate her on occasions, and hounded this little interloper who dared to infringe on their grazing grounds. Luckily, Susie easily out-distanced them.

About a year after we acquired the curlew there was an unexpected development. Susie's wild friends had taken to venturing quite close in with her at feeding time. One of the wild birds in particular, hung around even during the day. At such close quarters we observed slight differences between the two birds. Susie had darker feathers around the eyes and head, while the other bird inclined to a lighter brownish colour. When she disappeared into the bush more often , we began to think Susie might bring us back a family of Bush curlews. Then a few days later Susie and friend were spied mating. 'Susie', we discovered was a boy!

Many of the Island's bird calls are difficult to identify at first, such as the trill of the colourful Rainbowbird or Bee-eater. Red-orange on his head, bright red eye, orange throat, yellow breast, green back merging to bright blue above his rump, and a dark tail decorated with two long central spine feathers, the whole effect enhanced by one or two appropriate black bands — how else could he be described, but as a rainbow? And the nick-name 'Bee-eater' is also well earned, for E. J. Banfield gave up keeping bees for honey on Dunk Is land, rather than slay the. 'rainbow'.

Most diminutive in size and sound is the tiny Sunbird, a mere three to four inches long, and often likened to the Humming-bird because of its habit of hovering over a flower for nectar. A bright yellow breast and long, curved honeyeater type bill distinguishes this little fellow, the male having a dark-blue, almost black throat. The rapid, canary-like notes are heard from close-up when a pair not infrequently favours a houseowner by building its long, dangling nest from a corner of his verandah. The completely enclosed nest, with side entrance, has a long tail-piece of cobwebs and grass, making it look for all the world like a piece of bark from a tree caught up in the breeze on a thread.

Susie the curlew

The Swamp pheasant or Coucal is a mostly unseen melodian, with his mysterious "Coop, coop, coop, coop,1 from the depths of the forest. Occasionally though, this long-tailed, brown speckled bird will reveal himself on the grass flats, fluttering awkwardly along just above ground level.

The great white, Sulphur-crested cockatoo leaves no doubt as to his identity, as he flies overhead at any hour of the day or night, uttering a deafening screech. Rainbow Lorikeets, which always manage to arrive in a flock, never fail to announce their presence with a very noisy chattering among the gum-blossoms.

But as in human society, there are quieter, more sedate members of the fraternity. From October to April the migratory Torres Strait pigeon, or Nutmeg pigeon as Banfield called him, comes down for the Wet Season. A beautiful white bird with dark-brown, almost black wing-tips and tail, and a body slightly larger than the ordinary pigeon. A defined whirring of wings (a peculiar characteristic of all pigeons), will be heard as they fly swiftly up into Gustav Valley, their favourite haunt.

Other pigeons are well represented: the Green-winged pigeon and the smaller, multi-coloured Purple-crowned pigeon, as well as Peaceful doves. We found a dead Purple-crowned pigeon under a tree in the bush one day — a completely dried out skin with all its colourful feathers intact, unmutilated, as good as a mounted specimen — the cause of death unknown. We preferred to think of it as just old age .

On another occasion we had the satisfaction of saving the life of a little songster. A thirsty Forest Kingfisher had flown down into the pony's drinking trough, unable to get out when his feathers became water-logged. It was unfortunate that the make-shift trough, an old clothes copper, was only one third full of water at the time, its steep edge preventing the bird's escape. The weather had been very hot and dry for some weeks, so we understood his predicament, but only arrived in the nick of time. The children saw him first, but his ferocious looking, over-sized beak, squawked at them wide open and menacingly every time they attempted a rescue. They called me and I ran down to find him all but exhausted, floundering on the water surface with big beak open and panting. That same strong beak latched firmly onto my fingers with a force surprising for the size of the bird (he was only six inches long), as I reached down to haul him out. After I persuaded him to give me back my finger, he uttered a shrill, trilling protest, the same familiar call of his kind, and we admired his pluckiness . It was a thrill to hear his loud clear voice at such close quarters, and to get a first hand view of his beautiful, bright-blue plumaged back. I held him quietly for a quarter of an hour or so , allowing him to spread his wings until the feathers dried in the hot sun, then released him. One more rude farewell squawk, and he shot straight as an arrow for the nearest high tree. After this, we installed a permanent shallow bird-bath — a safer refuge for our flying friends.

A list of bird species, permanent and migratory on Magnetic Island, has been prepared by the Townsville Bird Observers Club and others, who have reported sightings of no less than 189 different birds. The list appears at the end of this chapter. A few of the more common ones are the Butcher-bird, Fig-bird, Grey Fantail, Spangled Drongo (Fish-tail), White-breasted Woodswallow, Welcome swallow, Grey swiftlet, occasional Black crows and Wedge-tailed eagles, and a few honeyeaters and flycatchers. Introduced birds are fortunately fairly rare such as the Indian Mynah and the house sparrow, common in Townsville just across the water. The mynah seems to prefer human company to the wildness of the bush.

There are many sea birds around the Island, most notable being the Brahminy Kite. These immaculate birds, with rust-red back and shoulders and pure white head and breast, often come well inland on a windy day "to soar above the forest clearings in search of prey. The brown feathered Osprey, or Fish-hawk, build their huge stick nests in prominent positions on many of the rocky headlands around Magnetic. Terns, Seagulls, Beach-curlews and little Sea-dotterels inhabit the beaches.

There is a large freshwater lagoon just back from the foreshore in Horseshoe Bay which has attracted many water birds to the Island, including at one time the graceful Native Companion or Brolga. Standing over a metre high with its long crane-like neck, it is, like the Jabiru, one of our largest birds, with a wing-span of two metres. The light-grey, almost white body is relieved by a delicate orange-coloured head marking. It is of course well known for its dancing performances, which so endeared it to the Australian Aborigines. The Dreamtime legends of the latter say that it was once a beautiful girl called Bralgah, who, because she did nothing else but dance all day long, was finally turned into a bird. The Brolga stands for long periods balanced on one leg, a feat also imitated by the Aboriginal. In spite of its ungainly running take-off, it is a powerful flyer, being able to cover long distances — between the mainland and the Island, for instance.

The Jabiru, or black-necked stork, found on the same lagoon, has a larger head and longer bill than the Brolga, with a dark-green, almost black sheen to its head and neck feathers. It is Australia's only native stork, just as the Brolga is our only crane.

The Nankeen Night-heron is an unusual visitor. The dense foliage of a mango tree is often a refuge during daylight hours for one of these big birds, a tell-tale pile of crab-shells and fish-bones lying on the ground under his perch.

There is no more Australian sound than the laugh of the Kookaburra, and there are plenty on Magnetic. Apart from the scream of the weeloo, the night hours are punctuated by the repetitive call of the Boobook owl or Mopoke, a familiar sound in many parts of Australia. In some areas the Hammer-bird or White-tailed nightjar makes his monotonous, "Chop, chop, chop, chop," for hours on end through the night. Then just before dawn comes the cackle of the scrub fowl, which builds huge mound nests to incubate its eggs.

But above all the myriad sounds of the tropic night- the grunt of koalas, cussing of possums, croak of green tree-frogs, beeping of geckoes, singing of crickets, thumping tail of rock-wallabies, and the monotonous mopoke — above all this sound of a wild, nocturnal life, the distant mournful wail of a bush curlew will penetrate to the farthest grove. It is the sound of an ancient isle, of ages past, of the Aboriginal Dreaming. The weeloo is surely the voice of Magnetic.

***

List of Birds seen on Magnetic Island, compiled from information supplied by Carine Williams and Andree Griffin of the Wildlife Preservation Society of Old, and Jo Wieneke of Nelly Bay.

Bittern, Black
Booby, Brown
Brolga
Bronzewing, Common
Brush Turkey
Bush Hen
Bush Lark
Butcher-bird, Pied
Cicada bird
Cisticola,
    Golden-headed
Cockatoo, Sulphur-crested
    Red-tailed black
Cockatiel
Coat, Australian

Corella, Little
Cormorant,
    Black
    Little black
    Little pied
    Pied
Crow, Australian (Torresian)
Cuckoo,
    Black-eared
    Brush
    Channel-billed
    Fan-tailed
    Golden bronze
    Horsfield bronze
    Oriental

Pallid
Rufous-breasted bronze
Cuckoo-shrike, Black-faced Curlew,
Beach (Stone curlew)
Bush (Stone curlew)
Eastern
Currawong, Pied
Darter
Dollar-bird
Dotterel,
Black-fronted
Double-banded
Mongolian sand
Red-capped
Dove
Bar-shouldered
Emerald
Peaceful
Drongo, Spangled
Duck,
Black
Water whistling
White-eyed
Eagle,
Wedgetailed
Whistling (kite)
White-breasted sea-
Egret,
Little
Plumed
White (Large)
Falcon,
Little
Peregrine
Fantail,
Grey
Northern
Rufous
Black & white (Willie Wagtail)

Figbird, Yellow (hybrid)
Fig-parrot, Double-eyed
Finch
Chestnut-breasted (Mannikin)
Double-barred
Flycatcher,
Black-faced
Leaden
Restless
Satin
Shining
Spectacled (Monarch)
White-eared (Monarch)
Frair-bird,
Helmeted
Frigate-bird, Lesser
Galah
Gannet, Brown, (Booby)
Godwit, Bar-tailed
Black-tailed
Goshawk,
Australian (Brown)
Grey (White)
Grassbird, Tawny
Grebe, Little
Greenshank
Gull, Silver
Harrier, Spotted
Hawk,
Collared sparrow-Crested
Heron,
Mangrove
Nankeen night-Reef
White-faced
Honeyeater,
Blue-faced
Brown-backed
Dusky
Ibis,

Straw-necked
White
Jabiru
Jacana,
Comb-crested (Lotus bird)
Kestrel, Nankeen
Kingfisher,
Forest
Little
Mangrove
Red-backed
Sacred
White-tailed
Kite,
Black
Black-shouldered
Brahminy
Whistling
Koel, Indian
Kookaburra,
Laughing
Blue-winged
Lorikeet,
Rainbow
Scaly-breasted
Magpie, Australian
Magpie lark (Mudlark)
Martin, Fairy
Mistletoe-bird
Moorhen, Dusky
Mynah, Indian
Needle tail, white-throated
Nightjar, Long-tailed (White-tailed)
Noddy,
White-capped
Oriole, Olive-backed
Osprey (Fish hawk)
Owl, Boobook
Eastern Grass
Oystercatcher,
Pied
Sooty
Pardalote, Straited
Pelican, Australian
Petrel, Wilson's storm Southern Giant
Pheasant coucal
Pigeon
Brown
Domestic
Purple-crowned
Red-crowned
Topknot
Torres Strait
White-headed
Wompoo
Pitta, Noisy (Buff-breasted)
Plover,
Eastern gofden
Masked
Quail, Brown
Red-backed button
Rail, Banded land Rainbow-bird (Bee-eater)
Raven, Australian
Sandpiper,
Common
Sharp-tailed
Sandplover, Large
Scrub fowl (megapode)
Shearwater, Wedge-tailed
Shrike-thrush,
Rufous
Snipe, Japanese
Sparrow, House
Spoonbill,
Royal
Yellow-billed
Stilt, Pied
Stint, Red -necked

Sunbird, Yellow-breasted
Swallow, Welcome
Swamphen, Eastern
Swan, Black
Swift, Fork-tailed
Swiftlet, Grey
Tattler, Grey-tailed
Teal, Grey
Tern,
    Black-naped
    Bridled
    Caspian
    Common
    Crested
    Gull-billed
    Lesser-crested
    Little
Triller, Varied (Pied)
Turnstone, Ruddy
Warbler,
    Large-billed
    Mangrove
White-throated
Whim brei
Whimbrel, Little
Whistler,
    Golden
    Rufous
Wood-swallow, White-beasted
    White-browed
Wren, Red-backed

CHAPTER 9
MARINE LIFE

Magnetic Island lies wholly within the Great Barrier Reef Marine Park, the largest marine park in the world. The Island is zoned into various areas where some activities such as spearfishing are prohibited. These zones are described in detail in a brochure published by the Marine Park Authority.

The full wonder of the 2,000 kilometre long Great Barrier Reef could not possibly be presented in an aquarium. Yet at the Shark World marine gardens on Magnetic Island, a remarkable range of underwater life from the Reef has been brought on to land, displayed in large glass tanks at convenient eye-level viewing positions like a living, pulsating art gallery of nature. Sights usually only the privilege of an underwater skin-diver are here shown close-up for everyone to see. The tanks, lit with fluorescent lamps, reveal the full colours of a seething wonderland of variety and form which only nature could dream up.

The unusual fact here is that it is *all* alive, even to the brilliantly coloured corals pulsating and wavering with the water movement, made possible because of the 'open-circuit' type water circulation employed.

This system supplies completely clean natural sea-water flowing through the tanks and constantly draining back to the sea, forming an environment which is essential to live corals because they exist on plankton, minutest life in the sea . Many aquariums world-wide operate either on a fully 'closed-circuit' system where air is artificially supplied, or by partial recirculation of sea-water only. Corals gradually die under such conditions, whereas at the Magnetic Island acquarium the corals not only live, but actually reproduce themselves as well.

One of the founders and long time manager of this unique acquarium, New Zealander Ian Croll, an experienced skin-diver, captured most of the early specimens for the tanks. Ian left New Zealand in 1958 for a three month holiday in the tropics, spending a few weeks diving at New Caledonia before going on to Green Island off Cairns. But he didn't get back home. Ian spent eight years on Green Island with Vince Vlasoff who established the Marineland there. The Magnetic Island venture opened in 1967 with three partners — Ian Croll, Vince Vlasoff and Fred Paterson, a retired engineer from Townsville.

Of all the islands along the Barrier Reef coastline, Magnetic was considered eminently suitable for a project of this size, because of its accessibility to the mainland and the constant stream of daily visitors. Pleasantly sited in a quiet corner at the southern end of Nelly Bay beach, and adjacent to Rocky Bay over the small peninsula where the manager's home overlooks the Gardens, the surrounds are nicely landscaped with spacious lawns, palm trees and flowering shrubs, and barbecue facilities under the sheoak trees near the clean sandy beach.

The most spectacular part of the display is the larger tanks of coral and fish in the main hall, some of them 30 feet long, of three-quarter inch plate glass, containing over 4,000 gallons of constantly changing sea-water, constructed in a long, narrow form to present an optimum view of the contents.

The so-called 'soft' corals (Aicyonarians) are favoured as exhibits because of their better reproductive qualities, and also because their ' live' movement in the water currents makes a more spectacular display. Most of the true stony type corals extend their polyps or tentacles only at night, during which time the plankton is more active for feeding. In daylight they appear mostly as hard, unattractive masses; however, some of them do extend in patches during the day.

It is now generally well known that the coral polyp is a simple form of animal life very like a sea anemone, but with the added power of forming a calcium carbonate skeleton. The polyp itself is a tiny fleshy tube, with a group of even smaller tentacles at the top which can be quickly retracted if disturbed. Their method of feeding is one of the miracles of nature which can be observed only under a microscope. In the fleshy part of the polyp tentacles are numbers of minute, barbed stinging capsules (known to scientists as Nematocysts) which may be likened to a coiled spring held down by a small delicate, inflated rubber bulb. When small particles of sea life brush against the tentacles of the polyp, the 'rubber' bulb is punctured , thus re leasing the innumerable microscopic threads or barbs which inject venom into the prey, sufficiently potent to immobolize it immediately. The food is then passed to the polyp mouth, either by the tentacles or by water currents.

The very active soft corals feed during the day and are therefore more popular with visitors because of their more colourful display at this time, but unlike the hard corals they do not possess a limy skeleton. When they die they just disintegrate, playing virtually no part in the great reef-building process. The stony coral reef-builders, such as the well known brain-coral and staghorn-coral, are less hardy and flourish only in shallow water at temperatures not below 68 degrees F, whereas many soft corals grow in deep water down to 20 fathoms, and are not so much affected by water temperature or excessive silt at the mouths of mainland rivers and so on. Nevertheless, numbers of the hard type corals are successfully displayed alive in the tanks, many showing only part of their polyp surface extended, the rest appearing as 'dead' coral, the polyp having retracted right into the hard base. One has only to return in an hour, however, to see the same coral fully extended in beautiful form, and hardly recognizable as the same piece. The rate of growth of coral is extremely slow, and it has been estimated that Queensland's Great Barrier Reef must have taken hundreds of thousands of years to form.

All coral exhibited at Shark World has been collected from around Magnetic Island. They range through Brain-coral, Rosette (bright red), Lettuce-coral, Red Harp-coral and Fern-corals, to fluorescent type corals which flourish in deeper water in crevices away from strong sunlight. Some of the latter actually prefer 'dirty' conditions like the reef at Picnic Bay, where many specimens have been taken even under the jetty. Many so-called 'dead' reefs such as in the Picnic Bay area, still have good patches down off the edges in deeper water. One or two of the corals, such as the Organ-pipe, do not, like most, bleach white when exposed to the sun, but retain their bright red colour indefinitely. Strangely, this coral when viewed alive down in the depths is actually a bright green colour, the live polyps completely camouflaging the red skeleton .

Coral on an actual reef may be viewed by taking the Reef Walk or Snorkel Trail at Geoffrey Bay during the lowest spring tides in winter. This is zoned as a 'Marine National Park B' area, where all line fishing and spearfishing is prohibited, and where nothing at all may be removed. Reef walking can be destructive to the environment due to trampling effects, therefore visitors should keep to the specially developed trail at the western end of Geoffrey Bay, as described in the Marine Parks brochure on 'Reef Walking'.

Also displayed are some less attractive members of the Reef world — the slimy-looking Beche-de-mer of which many varieties exist, including one very colourful member of the same family found locally and known as the Sea-cucumber. This latter has a blue-purple body colour with bright red stripes and edging marks along its often puffed-up shape. It walks along the sea bed with tiny, protruding red spikes. Various shells, including the world's largest bivalve shell-fish , the Giant Clam, can be seen in the tanks. The Clam can grow up to four feet in length and weigh up to 500 pounds, but it does not catch fish or deli berately trap deep-sea divers as some would have us believe, for it feeds on minute sea life like the other shell-fish do. A definitely dangerous inhabitant of the stonier foreshores is the ugly, sluggish Stone-fish, which blends almost completely into it surroundings in the bottom of one of the smaller tanks at the aquarium. Its real colour is a greenish-marbled toning, but when found naturally it is covered with a coating of dirty slime corresponding in colour to the surrounds. The Stone-fish possesses an unlucky thirteen strong dorsal spines, all of which are provided with a poison-sac and, if trodden on, can cause death.

The largest of the fish displayed in the big tanks are the Queensland Groper. Specimens weighing 50 to 60 pounds look big enough, but they do grow in excess of 800 pounds. With their enormous mouths and inquisitive nature these oversized Cod are very much respected by pearl-divers, for it is claimed that men have been swallowed whole by them. Although in their natural state they prey on smaller fish, one of the amazing things about the aquarium is that dozens of small colourful fish swim freely side by side unmolested by the Groper. In this happy colony of well-fed inmates who become accustomed to each other, harmony is complete. Every fish knows his place and behaves himself, even two Black-tip whaler-sharks. Occasionally at feeding time, though, the young sharks have been known to get excited and snap at other fish — mostly at the poor old Puffer-fish who has teeth sunk unceremoniously into his tail during this outburst of the 'pack-feeding' instinct.

The normal harmony in the aquarium even extends between fish and the deadly sea-anemone, which has polyps similar to coral, only larger. Ian says that the little red Decoy-fish which hover among the Anemone tentacles unharmed, fail to fool any of the other fish, who know all about old Anemone and won't go near. But the Anemone exists on minute organisms in the water.

Trouble comes when new fish are introduced into the tanks. They would quickly disappear if it were not for the special introductory 'fence' — a screen inserted across one end of the tank, through which the fish can see each other without molestation, while adapting to the colony. However, a big Groper, when first introduced and before learning his manners, took everyone by surprise. He was put in with two young sharks which were almost as long as the Groper himself, as it was thought they would be well able to look after themselves. Next morning the aquarium was minus two sharks — inside old Groper. Although he looks such a sleepy old fellow, half lying on his side, completely motionless most of the time, with tiny Cleaner-fish swimming unharmed in and out of his slightly open mouth picking out the parasites, he can be deceptively fast — fast enough obviously to catch two swift sharks in one night.

The Black-tip whaler-sharks grow to only seven feet in length, but can be quite nasty for their size. They are a well-proportioned shark and fairly aggressive. Other nasty customers to 'meet in the open ocean are the Sea-snakes, which are highly venomous, though not particularly efficient biters. One of these crawled over the top of its tank one night and perished in a crevice outside. One of the two original Octopus also took to changing his abode at leisure by crawling over the top and into adjoining tanks. He did it once too often however, and unable finally to get back, perished on the floor, Moray eels, with their nasty teeth, share a place with the Sea-snakes. One of these fellows took a hunk out of the backside of Ian's rubber diving-suit t he day it w as captured.

Some of the smaller fish are nearly as colourful as the coral environment they inhabit, the best example being the ornate Butterflycod or Fire-fish, in resplendent bright orange, red, and a little blue, completely covered with adorning striped spines. He is a slow swimming species whose dorsal spines are venomous like· the Stone-fish. One early specimen used to like live food , but had to be finally weaned of that habit because it was too much constant effort supplying him. He soon acquired more mundane tastes. Other colourful little beauties are the yellow and black striped Bat-fish, Harlequin Tusk-fish with gay stripes, the unusual Unicorn-fish with a horn protruding from its head, and the small, flat -shaped Cheatadons. There is also a rare Moorish-idol fish, popular subject of the artist's brush, which needs plenty of room and is difficult to keep in captivity. Game fish are included, such as the Barramundi, Silver Trevally, Sweet-lip, Red Emperor, Coral trout and Coral cod.

At one end of the aquarium, beyond the main series of tanks, is the wide, open Turtle pool, artistically designed with curves and ornamental green shrubs here and there on the edges. A big Green-turtle four feet across, weigh£ three hundredweight. This species is common around Magnetic Island, as is the Hawksbill-turtle. Recent research by zoologists has indicated that the heart-beat of a turtle is much slower when he submerges; only one beat per minute, enabling him to stay under for up to half an hour at a time. An unusual feature of the Turtle pool is the Sucker-fish which attach themselves to the shells of Mama and Papa turtle as they swim through the clear water, with baby turtle hovering just beneath the big protecting bulk of Mama. The Sucker-fish, which cling on with a sucker-disc on their heads, are not parasites, but merely go along for the ride, and to feed on rubbish left after the turtle has been feeding.

An interesting sight is feeding time in the tanks. Ian always left this chore until late afternoon, allowing the corals to make use of some of the minute particles during the hours of darkness. The food was a mixture of prawns, shell-fish, sardines, mullet, mince-meat, ox-heart and kidneys, all minced up and kept frozen for ready use. Big chunks of cod or trout and some whole fish serve the gropers and sharks. Ian allowed me to watch one evening as he did the rounds . While Ian was outside, lifting the tank covers one at a time to drop in some food , I watched fascinated through the glass walls inside.

At the very first tank, housing Painted crayfish and Toad-fish, there was a sudden stirring of interest and all eyes focussed toward the surface as the cover was lifted to reveal full daylight. The fat Toad-fish swam toward the surface even before the first chunks of meat were dropped in — they all knew it was supper-time. In one second a chunk of food floated slowly down in front of Toadie's nose; next instant it had disappeared in a lightning grab. As other chunks fell to the bottom, two of the biggest crayfish gently scooped up one or two pieces underneath their bodies, cradling them towards the mouth with those innumerable small legs of theirs, while they went to work slowly digesting the food with oscillating mandibles.

A similar interest was displayed by the inmates of most of the other tanks as the lid was lifted , except for the big groper. He doesn't like to be watched when fed. He could see me through the glass, and just lay there motionless in his peculiar half-tipsy position near the bottom, one big eye cocked sideways watching a falling hunk of meat. Then the big eye swivelled in its socket to observe me again, his body still motionless. After a full minute of deliberation, the old groper slowly moved forward, twisted slightly more on his side, then while still two or three inches from the piece of food, opened his cavernous mouth and sucked. Pieces large and small disappeared into that great cavity in one draw; all with a very minimum of effort by the monster.

A few minutes later the other groper in the tank opposite started into instant life as the cover was lifted, swimming the full length of the thirty foot tank in a second, as if to belie the sleepy impression his cousin had made, and I remembered those unfortunate sharks.

Stinging Jelly-fish or Sea-wasps have long been a subject of interest in tropical waters, due mainly to the several human fatalities caused by contact with their tentacles. Every year between November and April during the Monsoon, this menace is present in waters north of latitude 26"S. The Sea-wasp, or Box Jelly-fish, has a cuboidal or bell-shaped, translucent body, nearly colourless, with long pendulous tentacles protruding from four corners, sometimes up to 30 feet in length. Its sting is very potent and when it touches the skin is like a red-hot poker, leaving a weal the full length of contact, which if not rapidly treated can cause death. The biggest danger lies in the fact that the Jelly-fish prefer close inshore waters; and in particular, murky waters, which often occur with a northerly wind in summer, stirring up the bottom silts. They are difficult enough to see in clear water, so under these conditions it is not surprising that some people are stung every year. Magnetic Island is fortunately placed in this regard, eight kilometres off shore, as sea currents mostly seem to sweep them past the Island beaches onto the mainland.

With the continuing controversy on the Crown of Thorns Starfish along the Great Barrief Reef, one could not visit the aquarium without taking a close look at the unpopular subject itself, sitting unconcernedly in one of the smaller tanks. It has a multi-radialled star form, each radial covered with myriads of sharp spines almost like a porcupine. The spines are poisonous with a sting similar to that of the sea-urchin. The Crown of Thorns publicity stems from its habit of consuming coral reefs all over the Pacific area . Some scientists have advocated drives to wipe out the Star-fish before it ruins reefs to the extent of endangering the actual existence of many coral islands. They say that the destroyed reef will no longer be able to act as a barrier to the encroaching sea, eventually causing total destruction of an atoll.

However, nature operates on a grand scale. She surely has her balance still under control in the long run, for the effects and side-effects are often far reaching, and not fully understood by man. Ian Croll's views on the subject are worth noting, as he has spent far more time exploring the reef than some theorists keen on expounding their views. After years of reef diving, I an said that the Crown of Thorns Star-fish has always been present, and in parts near Green Island previously eaten out, the coral is now building up again. But coral growth is a slow business and Ian said, "In some places the build-up is not as rapid as we'd like to imagine, but this is Nature taking its course. It's no good getting all excited and saying we'll have to wipe out the Crown of Thorns, because we don't know enough about them yet. It's probably a pity that they do wipe out a reef, but I still say, leave them alone."

An unfortunate property of the Star-fish is that if mutilated while still on the Reef, severed parts of the body can regenerate a new central disc and grow missing rays, adding even more to the population. But like grass-hopper plagues on the mainland, these effects do not last forever, and as far as coral regeneration is concerned, nature is a slow worker. Let us tread warily in unknown waters.

***

DUGONG

The Dugong (scientific name *Dugong Dugon*) is one of the most interesting marine creatures found in Magnetic Island waters. They are the 'cattle of the sea', being herbivorous mammals which graze on 'sea grass' beds in relatively shallow coastal waters, and like the cow suckle their young 'calves' with milk. A further parallel exists, for they are a valuable source of protein which is why they have become rare along the coasts of East Africa and southern Asia, the only other areas where they are found. Northern Australian waters now contain the main reservoir of dugong in the world, because of laws protecting them from commercial exploitation, and the always low human population density in this area.

However, during the past few years a new threat to their existence has arisen. With the rapid growth of tourism on islands like Magnetic, it has been felt necessary to protect the ever increasing swimming public from danger of attack by sharks, and many of the beaches have been netted. The nets used to protect Picnic Bay, Nelly Bay, Alma Bay and Horseshoe Bay are about 300 metres long, by 5 metres deep, with a 500 mm mesh. Drum lines with 200 mm baited hooks on chain traces are also used to catch Tiger sharks, Black-tip sharks, Whaler sharks, Tawny sharks and Hammer-head sharks. But along with the sharks, many other harmless animals fall victim — turtles, dolphins, harmless sharks, rays and large fish as well as the dugong, which are caught in the nets and drowned.

Dr George E. Heinsohn (Ph.D. Berkeley, California), of the Department of Zoology at James Cook University of North Queensland, has made a study of the dugong for a number of years, and the writer is indebted to him for the following information.

During the first year of netting on the main beaches of Magnetic Island in 1964-65, as many as 82 dugong were drowned. Since then the yearly fatality rate has fluctuated between 6 and 16, apart from a surge immediately after cyclone 'Althea' in 1971-72, when 41 were caught. Dr Heinsohn believes that most of the established local breeding population was wiped out in the very first year, thus accounting for the much lower figures for succeeding years. But he has also suggested (in order to explain the higher proportion of young dugong caught later) that older, more experienced dugong may become wary of the nets after associating their presence with the distress signals of a drowning mate; a hopeful thought for their preservation if they do 'learn' of another hazard in their environment.

Following the earlier fatalities, Dr Heinsohn arranged for all dugong specimens caught to be recorded for future study, and this has resulted in some gain in scientific knowledge of the species. For instance, he has discovered from an examination of the reproductive tracts and organs of females and males, that both sexes do not reach maturity until they are about 2.4 metres in body length. New born dugong are about 1.1 metres in length, and most births occur during August and September in this locality. The young calves accompany their mothers for more than a year after birth, and start eating sea-grass (in addition to milk) after about two to three months, just as a farm calf starts nibbling at about that age. They reach reproductive maturity at about 2 years of age.

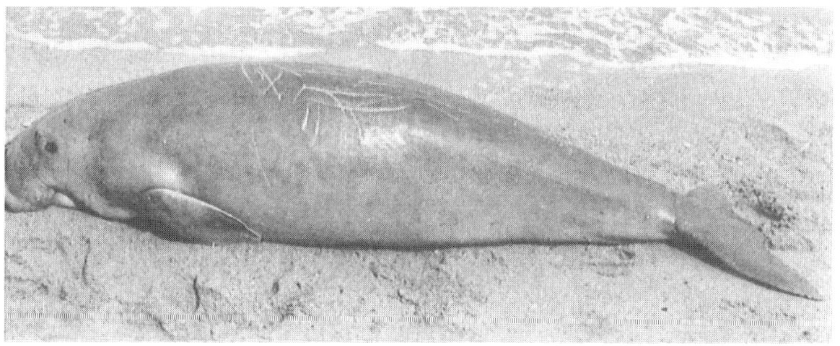

A dugong accidentally drowned in a fishing net. Dugong population around the Island has been severely decimated as a result of a government sponsored sharknetting programme. Photo: Dr G. E. Heinsohn

Most dugong netted have been caught at Picnic Bay, indicating a preference for feeding on shallow (under 5 metre) sea-grass beds between the Island and the mainland. Fewest dugong were taken from Alma Bay, where the water drops very quickly to larger depths and where the coast is most exposed to south-easterly winds. There is also naturally a generally reduced catch for the months of June and July, during the annual six week period of not setting nets.

During cyclone 'Althea' most of the nets were blown away or damaged beyond repair, and full netting was not resumed until several weeks later. Then during the four months following the cyclone, 23 dugong were caught and the monthly average for the rest of that year was much higher than normal to give the total of 41. Because of the larger number caught at Picnic Bay, that net was permanently removed in March 19?2 and replaced by baited hooks on drum lines.

Dr Heinsohn believes that alternatives to shark-netting must be considered as a long term conservation measure for dugong in the vulnerable coastal waters inside the Great Barrier Reef. The dugong has been totally protected by law in Queensland since 1969, except from Torres Strait Islanders and Aboriginal people who may hunt them for food. Drum lines are not a threat to marine mammals, but are not so effective in controlling dangerous sharks. The Tiger shark apparently likes the hooks, but without nets the baits could even encourage more sharks around beaches. Swimming enclosures would seem to offer the best solution to avoiding the appallingly high dugong fatalities, and would offer protection to the swimming public from the lethal Sea-wasp *Chironex fleckeri* as well.

In the meantime, complete legal protection is an absolute necessity, says Dr Heinsohn. The main chance for survival of the dugong as a species may even lie in their culture for meat, but this would require very much more scientific knowledge of their habits. A case exists for increased research into the ecology of the dugong. But if nets continue to be used, let us hope that there are still many old and wise Dugong Dugon around Magnetic Island who have learned by hard experience of one more danger lurking in their great ocean environment.

A resident at the Koala Park, Horseshoe Bay

CHAPTER 10
MODERN MAGNETIC TOURISM AND LATER SETTLERS

Various imaginative schemes have been advanced for further development on Magnetic Island, from the multi-million dollar dream of marina type settlement at West Point, to additional select tourist resorts in some of the less accessible and as yet untouched, quieter bays around the rugged coastline. Less popular, has been the suggestion of a causeway linking West Point with the mainland. This world at once remove the very essence of island living — a refuge cut off from the roar of mainland traffic — a sanctuary for flora and fauna, isolated from mainland predators. It would destroy the whole image of a Pacific island paradise, at present just nicely accessible at eight kilometres offshore, yet untouchable by the undesirable elements.

Tourism has grown along with the improvement in accommodation facilities on this, one of the biggest islands along the Reef coastline. Its size enables it to offer many things not available at other island resorts — golf course, tennis, bowls, mountain walks, secluded beaches and a full choice of the kind of accommodation desired, from flats, guesthouses, motels to hotels. There are horses to ride, bicycles, sailing catamarans and fishing boats for hire, as well as the facilities provided by many local sports clubs including Surf Life Saving Clubs and youth camps. Post Offices operate at some bays, and a State School at Nelly Bay. General food stores, newsagencies and souvenir shops have sprung up everywhere, including various restaurants.

***

A colourful backbone to the Island's transport system for many years was t he bus service, a series of old die-hard Chevrolet truck chassis with seats fitted on the tray under a shade canopy, which gave full 'air-conditioned' comfort in this climate. The buses, named 'Galloping Gertie', 'Nippie Nell', 'Flighty Flo', with later additions such as 'Modern Millie', added character to the Island roads as they chugged around the steep pinches, giving unrestricted view of an eye-catching coastline. Peter Mears came to Magnetic in 1960 to take over the bus service from Alf Armour, and covered the whole Island from Horseshoe Bay to Picnic Bay with a regular service. In the beginning, during the first days of motor cars in the 1920's and 30's, Eric Paskin ran a 1922 model Dodge truck converted for use as a bus, serving the Nelly Bay area only. No roads existed through to Arcadia, Horseshoe or Picnic then. Bill Svenson ran a separate bus in Horseshoe Bay, Charlie Gifford operated another in Arcadia, then Bob Hennequin and Bob Clark took over with a combined Arcadia-Horseshoe run soon after the Horseshoe Bay road was completed in 1939. In those days the primary function of the 'bus' was to carry freight. If there were many crates to be loaded, passengers just fitted in where they could. A visitor to the Island in August 1939 recorded that there were then 15 motor vehicles on the Island, and that it was possible to travel by motor car all the way from Horseshoe Bay to Hawkings Point (site of the present day Marine Gardens). and from Picnic Bay to the most distant point of the Isle, West Point, There remained only a link of about half a mile over the ridge between Picnic and Nelly Bays, to complete the Island motorway. This link was not opened until after the second World War, to convert the pleasant foot trail over the hills, known as 'Lover's Walk', into a motor road .

***

As the age of motor vehicles flourished and man's walking abilities declined, so it became necessary for a taxi service and drive-yourself vehicles on the big Island. Graham and Jo Wieneke pioneered a Mini-moke 'rent-a-car' service some years ago. Graham, an engineer graduate from Brisbane University, retired from the rat-race at an early age to build himself a trimaran and sail to Magnetic Island. In Townsville he met Jo, a school-teacher from Sydney driving around Australia in a Volkswagen beetle. They married, bought the historic 'Our Island Home' in Nelly Bay, and in 1967 began a rent-a-car service using Graham's old beat-up Holden, Jo's VW and a Mini-moke. The Mini-moke proved most popular, so they bought more Mokes and before long found themselves at the centre of another 'mini rat-race' here on their quiet old Island — thirty-odd Mokes, a staff of girls to run them, maintenance problems, jingling telephones and people everywhere. They sold out to try 'retiring ' for the second time.

Cabbies regularly meet Hayles' launches to transport tourists to their quarters. Taxi owners seem to come and go fairly frequently, but Geoff D' Argeavel was one who stuck it for nine years before retiring to his Koala Park Oasis at Horseshoe Bay. Geoff, keenly interested in native fauna, has been responsible for saving the lives of many koalas after fire on the Island. During his first year on Magnetic, he saw some pathetic sights in the bush, which made him decide to do something for the koalas. That year a severe bush fire burnt through the whole Island, and Geoff recalled walking with a friend through part of the fire area soon after it had burned. Noticing a bright glow in the fork of a blackened, smoking tree, they looked closer to make the horrifying discovery of the burning body of a koala, full of eucalyptus from its gum leaf diet, lending a full, red glow to its cremation. The following day while driving retired architect Ran Taylor to Picnic Bay, Geoff saw another bear on the roadside, badly burned. Ran suggested the best thing would be to put it out of its misery, but Geoff sa id no, he'd take it home to see if it might recover. It did, and since then he has saved dozens of koalas in his 'hospital' room, a special place where he feeds them plenty of fresh green leaves until they recover enough to be released back to the bush.

***

At Nelly Bay right on the foreshore, there was for many years an Outpatients' Clinic of the Townsville General Hospital, staffed by the heroine of the Althea cyclone, Sister Cecily Steptoe, whose plucky exploits at the height of the big blow were written up in *Reader's Digest*. The cyclone completely destroyed the old clinic in its exposed position, and Cecily moved to new premises farther inland after that. Serious hospital cases are usually taken to town on the ferries, although there is a helicopter available for airlifting emergency cases to the mainland.

Nippy Nell, one of Peter Mears' tourist buses, 1969

The original Clinic building was built by another Island character, the late Fred Hobarth, a world wanderer who finished up at Magnetic. He left Austria as a youth in 1928 to go to sea, but jumped ship at Port Adelaide in 1930. During those difficult depression years Fred humped a swag all over Australia, before settling in for a while with the first workers at the silver-lead mines at Mt Isa , Queensland Later he spent some years in Fiji and New Zealand, and served with the N.Z. Army forces in Europe during the war, before returning to Queensland to eventually settle on Magnetic. Fred's main interest was the sea and he would often be seen spear-fishing around the reefs off Nelly Bay, or talking boats with his great circle of Island friends. He built five boats on the Island — *Johe* I, II, III, IV and V, the name *Johe* being a combination of names of his two daughters, Josephine and Heidi. Fred was always a little shy about telling of his shark escape . One day he speared a four-foot shark while fifteen feet underwater off the local Nelly Bay reef. Struggling to hold the threshing shark on his spear, he pressed it close against his body while surfacing . Now the pair of shorts Fred wore that day had an unruly front zip, gaping wide open, and the shark in its last agonies latched on to a very tender part of Fred's anatomy. With shark's teeth fastened on grimly, and powerless to extricate himself, Fred slowly kicked his way to shore before he could open the shark's mouth. With blood everywhere and unable to treat the injury himself, a very red-faced Fred had three stitches inserted by the Clinic Sister.

Rocky Bay

In March 1988 Andy Frost made a most interesting archaeological discovery in Nelly Bay. At low tide while walking over an old coral lagoon bed out from the mouth of Gustav Creek, Andy found several Aboriginal stone tools lying in the sand. There were axes with ground edges, hammers and anvils, scrapers, flakes and blades, all made out of local basalt, quartz, chert and rhyolite, which have been dated by James Cook

University as at least 12,000 years old, while some are related to tool types 25,000 years old found in Arnhem Land. The tools are thought to have been washed down the beach slopes over a long period of time from old shell middens in sand dunes near the river mouth. It is to be hoped that any future development of Nelly Bay foreshore does not interfere with further research into this deposit, one of the most important coastal archaeological sites in Australia.

***

A famous old lady who came to live on Magnetic in her later years, and who died there aged 101, was Granny Emie Cole. Together with her son, Lieutenant-Commander George Cole (RNR retired), and his author wife Jean and family, Granny Emie, then aged 92, sailed from East Africa to New Zealand in a 40-foot trimaran beating against the Trade Winds. Jean Cole describes the voyage of the trimaran *Galinule* in her book *Trimaran Against the Trades*. George Cole built *Galinule* on his farm in Kenya between 1962 and 1965, when he was forced to sell his land upon that country's independence. Their trimaran course against the prevailing winds took them across the Indian Ocean from Mombassa on the East African coast, via the Seychelles, Cocos Keeling Islands, Christmas Island, Darwin, Thursday Island, the Great Barrier Reef, to Brisbane, and thence across the Tasman to New Zealand, where they arrived in December 1966. The family's original intention was to settle in Nelson at the northern end of the South Island, where they successfully completed the trimaran voyage and where Granny was hailed by the press for her daring. However, the climate in New Zealand proved too cold for them and they finally settled in Horseshoe Bay on the Island they had sailed past in the trimaran, there to keep bees and sell honey.

***

Horseshoe Bay, the largest of the Island bays, has at its eastern end another smaller beach known as the 'White Lady', named after White Lady Rock, the prominent natural feature atop the rocky section of coastline separating it from Horseshoe beach. The rock resembles the life-sized figure of a woman standing on the rocks looking out to sea. Birds were originally responsible for the white draping, which has lately been added to with white paint.

A recluse, Clarrie Scrivener, chose the serenity and privacy of White Lady Cove soon after he first saw it while on a cruise after the War. He recalled it was a hot, . summer afternoon as he walked up the beach through the line of graceful casuarina trees gently moving with the faintest breeze. This spot, with its old hut left after the War, immediately appealed to him as a refuge, having an air of complete detachment from the world, yet there was Horseshoe Bay settlement just across the water when he needed it. He took out a lease on the land and began his Robinson Crusoe existence, using a kayak canoe to skim across the mile of water to Horseshoe Bay for his mail and supplies. A few years ago he had a serious fall among the rocks behind his dwelling and lay there immobilized tor two days before he was discovered and removed to hospital.

Another man, Keith Bryson, settled at White Lady some time after Clarrie Scrivener, to establish an oyster farm in the bay. As a mackerel fisherman working out of Townsville, Keith took to sheltering in various bays around. Magnetic when strong sou'easters blew up, instead of hanging around port. He soon came to favour Horseshoe Bay, especially during the early boisterous months of the year. Living on board his old 34 toot boat *By Golly* for days at a time, Keith began to think about his future. Fishing at sea is a hard life as one gets older, and not being keen on taking a shore job, he thought about oysters. He had often picked natural oysters off the rocks around the Island and observed that cultivation should not be too difficult. So he took a lease on a block of land at White Lady, to use as a base to try his luck with three oyster leases off the beach.

Keith devised various methods of cultivation, the earliest being the stick method. Small squares of fibrolite were threaded on vertical wires separated by pieces of cut hose and hung from iron rails embedded in the bottom. A later method of support was a welded box frame used as a floating cradle about ten feet square and four feet high, with drum floats at each corner, inside which were strips of oyster plates as before. This floated just above the sea bed out of the mud and sand, enabling the whole grid to be brought ashore if necessary for both ease of inspection and for harvesting.

There are five species of oysters in these waters, the two dominant ones being the Milky and the Blacklip. The Blacklip is larger, so named for its thick lips with which it filters plankton food from the water. It grows deeper in the water than the smaller Milky oyster, and whereas twenty to thirty Milkies may be packed in a selling bottle, only eight to ten Blacklips will fit in the same space. The fatter growing Blacklip is the better variety for cultivation, both from the point of view of handling and for the table.

There were many problems to be overcome with tides, rough water, and fresh water pollution of the sea. In his travels as a fisherman, Keith took note of the conditions under which natural oysters lived in various spots like Hinchinbrook Channel and Orpheus and Palm Islands. He saw that cultivation would not be possible near streams along the Queensland coast, because the annual freshwater flush in the rainy season would kill them out. An offshore island seemed to offer the best way of ensuring continual saline water, but posed the problem of getting sufficient shelter from boisterous seas, while maintaining enough water current movements to keep temperatures down. Hot, shallow water can kill oysters or retard growth .

Keith's interest in oceanography led him to attend courses and discussion groups on the subject, in his role as member of the Fish Board and secretary of the fisherman's organization in Townsville. He formed the opinion that one of the main reasons for poor rains and severe fluctuations in sea life along the Barrier Reef during some years, is the abnormally heavy sou'easters then predominating. This air movement, coming from up to 2,000 miles away, brings a cold water mass onto the Reef. Recent American and Russian research showed that in order to bring a low pressure zone in to the coast for rainfall, the water temperature at the surface must be about 80 degrees F. If the water is too cold, monsoonal lows will not come in, accounting for poor wet seasons and relatively dead water, containing insufficient plankton and sea life. On the other hand, with offshore winds such as sou'westers or nor'westers, which occur when a cyclone comes close in to the coast, an up-welling occurs in the ocean, bringing up rich water, full of plankton , which can be seen in the deep blue colour of the sea and in the bright phosphorescence at night time. Keith noticed that after six weeks of sou'westers, for instance, his oysters grew more than they had in the previous six months. Keith pointed out the danger of oil pollution on the Great Barrier Reef, which poses a real threat to the area. Because of the 'lagoon' effect created inside the Reef, the water movement is largely limited to tides going back and forth between Reef and shore, without any strong oceanic currents to carry pollution away.

***

Colourful characters will no doubt continue to drift ashore on the Magnetical Island, but let us conclude with the story of a man who has seen many phases of life on the Isle, and who, though he spent many years away from its shores, succumbed at last to its quiet charm. Ken Jaffrey, well known naturopath in both Sydney and Townsville, first came to Magnetic Island in 1921 as a boy, to recuperate from an illness. With his mother he lived in one of the origin al little thatched cottages at Mandalay guest house, next to the creek in Nelly Bay. He recalled the Japanese boys working there in the long-house where meals were served. A feature of Nelly Bay in those days was the long, curving cat-walk from the jetty leading into 'Our Island Home' and Mandalay, along which passengers carried their own baggage past old Mr Bottiger's strange house in the sea. There were no roads, no electricity and no radio, so people had to make their own entertainment. Family get-togethers at night in the long-house were common, all with their musical instruments — mouth-organs, ukeleles, or a button accordian, for a session of Island music. Picnic Bay was the same, where Ken stayed at Butler's guest house on one occasion. Hayles and Butler's launches called in at all the bays then, enabling a visitor to take his pick. Arcadia had very little development at that time, but Horseshoe Bay was full of well known characters, Bill Svenson and George Apjohn among them.

About 1935, a naturopath named Arthur Hughes conducted a small sanitarium and organic farm at Nelly Bay, on the site occupied later by Gerry Walker, the real-estate agent. The original house was on high blocks, underneath which all the patients slept in mosquito nets, eating their meals at a pagola in the garden. Mr Hughes' practice was very successful and at this time Ken Jaffrey, who had spent many holidays on the Is land, decided to become a naturopath himself, working for a while with Mr Hughes before opening a clinic of his own in Townsville in 1939. In 1945 Ken went to Sydney to run a clinic at Manly and later at Hopewood Health

Centre, where he remained until retiring in 1967 to his old haunt. Magnetic. He bought a ten acre property on the Island — an old dairy farm owned by the Fin lays just across the road from the Presbyterian Church Youth Camp in Nelly Bay . There he developed an organic farm, growing fruits and vegetables using only organic manures. During his time south, Ken wrote several books on health, fasting, and natural foods, and also a book on musical instruments, Reed Mastery, dealing with the reed instruments such as the taragato, oboe, bassoon, clarinet, saxophone and bag-pipes.

Visitor Information

The major part of Magnetic Island is a National Park, controlled by the Queensland National Parks and Wildlife Service. Visitors should recognize that the Island's future well being is very much in their hands, dependent upon their individual caring attitude towards it. The Island also lies wholly within the Great Barrier Reef Marine Park, and this requires additional care by a visitor while yet enjoying all the environment' has to offer.

Most of the waters around Magnetic Island are zoned General Use 'A' by ,the Marine Park Authority. This provides for most reasonable uses, including shipping and trawling, but not mining, oil drilling, commercial spearfishing, or spearfishing with underwater breathing apparatus. The western mangrove forested side of the Isle and Nelly Bay are General Use 'B' zone, which is somewhat more restricted. Here trawling and general shipping are prohibited, as well as those activities not al lowed in General Use 'A' zone. Florence Bay and Radical Bay are both Marine National Park ·A' zone, which allows for recreational use, including limited line fishing (one line with one hook per person), but spearfishing and collecting are prohibited, as well as those activities not al lowed in General Use 'B' zone. The eastern part of Five Beach Bay, Balding Bay, and the whole of Geoffrey Bay are Marine National Park 'B' zone, which is the most restricted category on the Island. It is a 'look but don't take' zone, which provides for appreciation of areas in their relatively undisturbed state. All fishing and other activities which remove natural resources are prohibited.

The general rules for a visitor to Magnetic Island are as follows:

- Leave the Island as you found it. Do not interfere with native flora and fauna, and do not litter.
- Be careful with fire. Use only fireplaces provided. Note that there may be a complete fire ban in dry weather. Check with NPWS Ranger.
- Leave your pets at home.
- Camping is not permitted in the National Park. A private camping site is available at Horseshoe Bay.
- Swimming can be dangerous during the summer months, due to the presence of marine stingers.
- Contact the Ranger if bushwalking away from tracks. The Ranger is at Hurst Street, Picnic Bay- Phone (077) 78 5378.
- Observe Marine Park rules as outlined in the brochure 'Great Barrier Reef Marine Park, Central Section, Zoning Information', available from tourist authorities.

Transport

Fast passenger ferries operate on regular schedules from Townsville to both Picnic Bay and Arcadia on Magnetic Island. Timetables are available from the various operators.

Vehicular ferries also operate from Townsville to Magnetic Island on a regular schedule. Bookings are usually necessary.

On the Island, buses and taxis meet ferries. All day bus tickets are available allowing unlimited travel to all bays.

Hire-car 'Rent-a-Make' services are available at Picnic Bay and Arcadia. Also scooter hire and bicycle hire.

An early vehicular ferry unloading at the Arcadia ramp

Accommodation

The following is a guide only to the various kinds of accommodation available on the Island. For further information contact the Magnetic Island Tourist Association.

Resorts, Hotels, Motels, Flats, Hostels

Picnic Bay:	Magnetic Hotel Motor Inn
	Picnic Bay Holiday Flats
	YHA Hostel
Nelly Bay:	Latitude 19 Resort

	Shark World — Backpackers
	Camlachie Flats
	Uniting Church Camp and YHA Hostel
	J.O.F. Youth and Conference Centre
Arcadia:	Arcadia Holiday Resort
	Alma Den Beach Resort
	Dandaloo Holiday Units
	Brooke Haven Flats — Backpackers
	Loyang Flats
	Magnetic Retreat Flats
Horseshoe Bay:	Coolawin Holiday Flats
	Weemalah Family Flats
	Geoff's Place Holiday Resort
Radical Bay:	Radical Bay Resort — Motel and bungalow units

Places to Visit

Shark World marine gardens, Nelly Bay

Koala Park Oasis,Horseshoe Bay

The Forts — walking track off hill top between Arcadia and Horseshoe Bay

National Park walking tracks and lookouts

Reef Walk, Snorkel Trail, Geoffrey Bay- self guiding, follow brochure map only

Reef Link trips and cruises

The Craft Shop old school house, Picnic Bay

Activities

Catamaran, boat hire

Paddle boats

Scuba diving

Horse riding

Bicycle hire

Tennis courts

Social and Sports Clubs

Magnetic Island Country Golf Club

Magnetic Island Bowls Club

Magnetic Island Sports and Recreation, Horseshoe Bay

Surf Life Saving Club, Arcadia and Picnic Bay

R.S.L.

Lions

Senior Citizens Association

Restaurants and Snack Bars

All Bays

Post Offices and Banks

Picnic Bay and Arcadia

Schools

Nelly Bay State School

Magnetic Island Community Kindergarten

Emergency Services

Ambulance— phone 78 5225

Hospital Clinic — phone 78 5107

Police — phone 78 5270

Or dial 000

Further information may be obtained from:

Magnetic North Tourism Authority

PO Box 1777

Townsville, Queensland 4810, Australia

Phone: (077) 71 2724

Queensland Tourist and Travel Corporation

303 Flinders Street

Townsville, Queensland 4810

Phone: (077) 71 3077

ABOUT THE AUTHOR

James Porter was born in South Australia, and worked as an electronic engineer in telecommunications for some years in Australia and overseas. A love of nature, begun as a boy photographing birds in the mallee, later extended to canoeing in Arnhem Land, bushwalking in the Australian Alps and Southwest Tasmania, climbing mountains in Ethiopia and Papua New Guinea, and sailing in a 33 foot yacht to Fiji and New Zealand. While working in Townsville he and his family lived for three years on an old 14 acre pineapple plantation in Upper Gustav Creek, Nelly Bay, Magnetic Island. He has written several novels for young people, and another guide book on the Family Islands (the Dunk and Bedarra group, 100 miles north of Magnetic); also edited selections from the writings of E. J. Banfield. He is a member of the Australian Conservation Foundation.